Michael Miller

Sams **Teach Yourself**

# Wikipedia®

## in **10 Minutes**

**SAMS** | 800 East 96th Street, Indianapolis, Indiana 46240

## Sams Teach Yourself Wikipedia® in 10 Minutes

Copyright © 2010 by Pearson Education, Inc.

ISBN-13: 978-0-672-33123-7
ISBN-10: 0-672-33123-3

*Library of Congress Cataloging-in-Publication Data*

Miller, Michael, 1958-
  Sams teach yourself Wikipedia in 10 minutes / Michael Miller.
     p. cm.
  Includes bibliographical references and index.
  ISBN-13: 978-0-672-33123-7
  ISBN-10: 0-672-33123-3
  1. Wikipedia—Handbooks, manuals, etc. 2. Wikipedia. 3. User-generated content. 4. Electronic encyclopedias. 5. Social media. I. Title.
  AE1.5.M557 2010
  030—dc22
                                        2009031115

Printed in the United States of America

First Printing October 2009

### Trademarks

All terms mentioned in this book that are known to be trademarks or service marks have been appropriately capitalized. Sams Publishing cannot attest to the accuracy of this information. Use of a term in this book should not be regarded as affecting the validity of any trademark or service mark.

### Warning and Disclaimer

Every effort has been made to make this book as complete and as accurate as possible, but no warranty or fitness is implied. The information provided is on an "as is" basis. The author and the publisher shall have neither liability nor responsibility to any person or entity with respect to any loss or damages arising from the information contained in this book.

### Bulk Sales

Sams Publishing offers excellent discounts on this book when ordered in quantity for bulk purchases or special sales. For more information, please contact

> **U.S. Corporate and Government Sales**
> **1-800-382-3419**
> **corpsales@pearsontechgroup.com**

For sales outside of the U.S., please contact

> **International Sales**
> **international@pearson.com**

**Associate Publisher**
Greg Wiegand

**Acquisitions Editor**
Katherine Bull

**Managing Editor**
Kristy Hart

**Project Editor**
Andy Beaster

**Copy Editor**
San Dee Phillips

**Indexer**
Lisa Stumpf

**Proofreader**
Jennifer Gallant

**Technical Editor**
Vince Averello

**Publishing Coordinator**
Cindy Teeters

**Designer**
Gary Adair

**Compositor**
Gloria Schurick

# Table of Contents

# About the Author

**Michael Miller** has written more than 90 nonfiction books over the past two decades. His best-selling titles include *Sams Teach Yourself YouTube in 10 Minutes, Absolute Beginner's Guide to Computer Basics, Googlepedia: The Ultimate Google Resource,* and *Speed It Up! A Non-Technical Guide for Speeding Up Slow Computers.* He has established a reputation for practical advice, technical accuracy, and an unerring empathy for the needs of his readers. For more information about Mr. Miller and his writing, visit his website at www.molehillgroup.com or email him at wiki10@molehillgroup.com.

# Dedication

*To Sherry: Another ten minutes, please?*

# Acknowledgments

Special thanks to the usual suspects at Sams, including but not limited to Greg Wiegand, Katherine Bull, Andy Beaster, and technical editor Vince Averello.

# We Want to Hear from You!

As the reader of this book, *you* are our most important critic and commentator. We value your opinion and want to know what we're doing right, what we could do better, what areas you'd like to see us publish in, and any other words of wisdom you're willing to pass our way.

You can email or write me directly to let me know what you did or didn't like about this book—as well as what we can do to make our books stronger.

*Please note that I cannot help you with technical problems related to the topic of this book, and that due to the high volume of mail I receive, I might not be able to reply to every message.*

When you write, please be sure to include this book's title and author as well as your name and phone or email address. I will carefully review your comments and share them with the author and editors who worked on the book.

E-mail: consumer@samspublishing.com

Mail: Greg Wiegand
Associate Publisher
Sams Publishing
800 East 96th Street
Indianapolis, IN 46240 USA

# Reader Services

Visit our website and register this book at www.informit.com/title/9780672331237 for convenient access to any updates, downloads, or errata that might be available for this book.

# Introduction

Wikipedia is a terrific resource, an online encyclopedia full of information about almost any topic you can imagine. What makes Wikipedia different from other encyclopedias, however, is that it's collaborative; all articles are written and edited by other users, just like you.

But how do you find the information you're looking for on the Wikipedia site? How do you know if what you read in Wikipedia is accurate? How do you edit articles you find that need elaboration? And how do you write a new article on a topic you know a lot about?

Well, that's where this book comes in. *Sams Teach Yourself Wikipedia in 10 Minutes* is a quick-and-easy way to learn how to find, read, and edit Wikipedia articles. Every lesson in this book is short and to the point, so you can learn everything you need to learn at your own pace, in your own time. Just follow the straightforward *Sams Teach Yourself in 10 Minutes* game plan: short, goal-oriented lessons that can make you productive with each topic in 10 minutes or less.

## What You Need to Know Before You Use This Book

How much prior experience do you need before starting this book? Absolutely none! You don't need to be a professional researcher or an academic. All you need is a computer with an Internet connection and a web browser. Everything you need to know flows from there.

## About the *Sams Teach Yourself in 10 Minutes* Series

*Sams Teach Yourself Wikipedia in 10 Minutes* uses a series of short lessons that walk you through the various aspects of Wikipedia and its companion sites. Each lesson is designed to take about 10 minutes, and each is limited to a particular operation or group of features. Most of the instruction is presented in easy-to-follow numbered steps, and there are plenty of examples and screen shots to show you what things look like along the way. By the time you finish this book, you should feel confident in both reading an editing articles on the Wikipedia site.

# Special Sidebars

In addition to the normal text and figures, you find what we call *sidebars* scattered throughout that highlight special kinds of information. These are intended to help you save time and to teach you important information fast.

---

**PLAIN ENGLISH**

Plain English sidebars call your attention to definitions of new terms. If you aren't familiar with some of the terms and concepts, watch for these special paragraphs.

---

**CAUTION**

Cautions alert you to common mistakes and tell you how to avoid them.

---

**TIP**

Tips explain inside hints for using Wikipedia more efficiently.

---

**NOTE**

Notes present pertinent pieces of information related to the surrounding discussion.

---

# Getting to Know Wikipedia

*In this lesson, you learn the history of Wikipedia and how it works.*

## Welcome to the World of Wikis

Wikipedia is, for many users, the primary site for information on the Web; it uses the concept of wikis to create an online encyclopedia. Hence the name, a combination of "wiki" and "encyclopedia."

But what is a wiki?

## How Wikis Work

In essence, a *wiki* is a collaborative database. That is, different users enter data into the database, and the database becomes a source of information for other users.

What makes a wiki different from a normal database is its collaborative nature. Instead of a single monolithic author, wikis have dozens or hundreds or even thousands of different authors, each contributing his or her own expertise to the enterprise. In this fashion, a wiki can quickly grow to encompass all manner of information, using the power of its multiple contributors.

A wiki becomes even more functional when connected to a network—or to the Internet. Any user with a network or Internet connection can access the wiki database, either to retrieve information or add data to the database. This broadens the base of contributors, which broadens the potential information available.

To facilitate data entry and formatting, most wikis use some type of markup language, such as the Web's HTML, for their data entry. Entries are created using the markup language so that all the data shares the same look and feel.

The markup language also enables different entries within the database to link to one another, and to other pages on the Web. In effect, wiki entries—called *articles*—are their own pages on the larger wiki website. By linking to other articles, a wiki article gains breadth and depth; one piece of information easily leads to related information elsewhere in the wiki.

## Wiki History

The first web-based wiki was launched by computer programmer Ward Cunningham in 1995. The WikiWikiWeb (www.c2.com/cgi/wiki/) was created to ease the exchange of ideas between programmers. Cunningham based the site's design on Apple's HyperCard application, which was a graphical database program included with Macintosh computers in the late 1980s. WikiWikiWeb featured user-modifiable pages that essentially created the collaborative database of information.

> NOTE: **Wiki Wiki**
>
> The word *wiki* is actually a Hawaiian word that means "fast." Ward Cunningham appropriated the word for his first collaborative database, remembering an employee at the Honolulu International Airport who told him to take the "wiki wiki" shuttle bus between terminals.

Users of the site embraced the concept and began to create their own wikis independent of the WikiWikiWeb website. These wikis focused on content other than programming, using wiki engines to create knowledge bases in various content areas. The most notable of these new wikis was a general purpose site, dubbed Wikipedia.

# Wikipedia: The World's Largest Encyclopedia

Programmer Ben Kovitz had worked with WikiWikiWeb, and on January 2, 2001, introduced it to Larry Sanger. At the time, Sanger was a software developer for a company called Bomis and was working on an online encyclopedia dubbed Nupedia. The Nupedia project didn't get off the ground, but Sanger saw that the wiki concept could be used to create an even more inclusive Web encyclopedia. Sanger suggested to Jimmy Wales, Bomis' owner, that they use a version of the UseModWiki engine that drove WikiWikiWeb to create their own wiki encyclopedia, which they eventually dubbed Wikipedia.

Wikipedia was formally launched on January 15, 2001. Initial articles came from previous Nupedia contributors, postings on the Slashdot technology news website, and sites found on major search engines. By the end of 2001, there were 20,000 articles in the Wikipedia database.

The site continued to grow in terms of readers, contributors, and number of articles. Wikipedia reached the 2 million article mark on September 9, 2007, which made it the largest encyclopedia ever assembled.

At present, Wikipedia hosts more than 2.9 million English-language articles, with a total of 13 million articles available in more than 250 different languages. The articles are written and revised by hundreds of thousands of individual contributors who volunteer their time and knowledge at no charge, for the good of the Wikipedia project.

The resulting knowledgebase is not only huge but also hugely popular. Wikipedia is the second-most searched site on the Internet, behind only Google. The site sees more than 10 million visitors each month, placing it among the top ten English-language sites on the Web.

# How Wikipedia Works

The Wikipedia site is found on the Web at www.wikipedia.org. To the casual user, Wikipedia looks and works like a traditional encyclopedia, albeit one based on the Internet. It's composed of individual articles, each focusing on a specific topic. Articles vary in length depending on the nature of the topic and the amount of information available.

Unlike a traditional encyclopedia, however, Wikipedia's content is created solely by the site's users; you don't have to be a professional or an academic to contribute articles to the site. Indeed, Wikipedia is used by people of all types, from students writing school papers to professional researchers to curious individuals.

The content on Wikipedia purports to present a neutral point of view; indeed, this policy of nonbias is codified as official site policy. However, there is no formal peer-to-peer process to review submitted articles; Wikipedia relies on its community of users to edit, correct, and police the information that other users create. After one user writes an article, other users can edit and add to that article. In this fashion, information is vetted for both accuracy and appropriateness.

The site's user/editors do follow broad editorial guidelines, however. These guidelines state that each entry must be about a topic that is encyclopedic and worthy of inclusion; this aims to avoid spurious topics that are not "notable," in Wikipedia's words. Entries must also expose knowledge that is already established or recognized; it cannot present independent works or new information not present elsewhere. Finally, entries should not reflect bias or take a side in a debate; all opinions and viewpoints should receive equal coverage within an article.

> NOTE: **Notable**
> According to Wikipedia's guidelines, a topic is *notable* if it has received significant coverage in mainstream media or academic journals that are independent of the subject of the topic.

Adding an article to Wikipedia is as easy as clicking a link and entering the article's text; articles can be accompanied by photographs and other media. Editing an article is equally easy because all edits are made directly to the main text of the article. Users who come across fraudulent, incorrect, or incomplete articles can report them to Wikipedia or simply edit the text in question in real time.

NOTE: **Creating and Editing**
Learn more about creating Wikipedia articles in Lesson 10, "Contributing a New Article"; learn more about editing articles in Lesson 9, "Editing an Existing Article."

Researching with Wikipedia is equally easy. The entire Wikipedia database can be searched from a simple search box; enter a keyword-based query and Wikipedia displays a list of matching articles. (Or in a more direct query, simply displays the appropriate matching article.) Articles include links to other Wikipedia articles and to outside websites; information referenced in each article is found in a series of footnotes at the bottom of the page.

NOTE: **Using Wikipedia**
Learn more about finding articles in Lesson 3, "Searching for Information"; learn more about individual articles in Lesson 4, "Reading a Wikipedia Article."

# Issues with Wikipedia

Because all Wikipedia content is user-generated and there is no central authority vetting or managing this content, some experts dismiss the usefulness of the site. Issues with Wikipedia fall into two general camps: accuracy and depth of coverage.

## Accuracy

If anyone can write or edit an article, how are you to know if the submitted information is accurate? Although the Wikipedia community is self-policing (and the information generally accurate), misleading or just plain wrong information can seep into the site. It is possible for mistakes to creep into Wikipedia's content and not be discovered by the base of contributing users—and for those mistakes to be reflected in papers and reports written with Wikipedia as the sole source.

## Depth of Coverage

Because Wikipedia users suggest the content, it's likely that some popular culture topics are more covered in more depth than topics of a more intellectual bent. This is solely a function of which and how many contributors are interested and expert in a given topic. As such, you can't depend on the Wikipedia to always provide adequate content.

## Beyond the Issues

With these issues in mind, it's best to view Wikipedia content as a start, rather than the final word when researching a topic. When you're writing a scholarly or professional paper, or just digging up information on a given topic, you should not use Wikipedia as your sole source, but rather as a guide to additional sources. In addition, it's always a good idea to check the footnotes and other references in a Wikipedia article to confirm the source of information presented; the most accurate articles are well sourced.

Despite the potential issues, Wikipedia remains the information source of first choice for millions of users. It's a great place to find information on just about any topic, from the highly academic to the casually popular. Whatever you're looking for, chances are someone else has written about it on Wikipedia.

> NOTE: **Researching**
> Learn more about researching with Wikipedia in Lesson 19, "Using Wikipedia for Research and School Papers."

# Other Wikipedia Sites

Wikipedia is part of the Wikimedia Foundation (www.wikimediafoundation.org). This nonprofit organization runs several other websites of interest to researchers and information gatherers. These sites are all based on the wiki concept and all dedicated to encouraging the development and distribution of free content to the public.

Wikimedia Foundation sites include the following:

- ► Wikimedia Commons (commons.wikimedia.org), a repository of free photographs, videos, music, and other media, discussed in Lesson 12, "Finding Pictures in the Wikimedia Commons"

- ► Wiktionary (www.wiktionary.org), a free multilingual dictionary, discussed in Lesson 14, "Looking Up Words in Wiktionary"

- ► Wikiquote (www.wikiquote.org), a collection of famous quotations, discussed in Lesson 15, "Finding Quotable Quotations with Wikiquote"

- ► Wikinews (wikinews.org), a free content alternative to commercial news sites, discussed in Lesson 16, "Getting the Latest News with Wikinews"

- ► Wikibooks (wikibooks.org), a database of free electronic textbooks, manuals, and public domain books, discussed in Lesson 17, "Reading and Editing Books Online"

- ► Wikisource (www.wikisource.org), a collection of classic books, laws, and other free works in a hypertext format, also discussed in Lesson 17

- ► Wikiversity (www.wikiversity.org), a project dedicated to learning materials and learning communities, also discussed in Lesson 17

- ► Wikispecies (species.wikimedia.org), a taxonomy database of species for scientific users

NOTE: **MediaWiki**
The Wikimedia Foundation also distributes the MediaWiki software, an engine used to develop new wikis. This open source software, available free of charge, has been downloaded more than one million times. Find out more at www.mediawiki.org.

As a nonprofit organization, the Wikimedia Foundation relies on the support of its users. (There are no ads anywhere on Wikipedia or related sites.) To donate, go to the Wikimedia Foundation website.

## Summary

In this lesson, you learned what Wikipedia is and how it works. In the next lesson, you learn to navigate the Wikipedia site.

# LESSON 2

# Navigating the Wikipedia Site

*In this lesson, you learn the main parts of the Wikipedia site—and how to find them.*

## Welcome to Wikipedia's Main Page

As you learned in Lesson 1, "Getting to Know Wikipedia," Wikipedia is a giant online encyclopedia, with all content contributed by the site's users. Articles are available in more than 250 different languages—and you get to these languages right from Wikipedia's home page.

The Wikipedia general home page is located at www.wikipedia.org. That's dot ORG, not dot COM—although entering www.wikipedia.com redirects to the correct page. As you can see in Figure 2.1, this page includes links to Wikipedia in different languages; click a language to go to the Wikipedia site in the language you want.

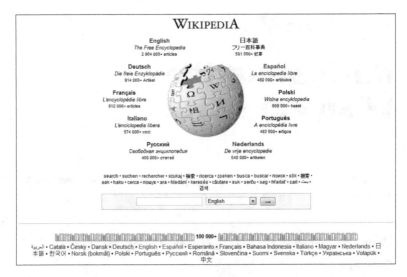

**FIGURE 2.1**    Wikipedia's multiple-language home page.

> NOTE: **Other Languages**
>
> Learn more about other versions of Wikipedia in the "Wikipedia in Other Languages" section, later in this lesson.

For our purposes, we assume you use the English-language Wikipedia site. To visit this site, click the English link on the upper-left side of the globe, or go directly to en.wikipedia.org.

You now see Wikipedia's English-language main page, as shown in Figure 2.2. This page includes the following sections:

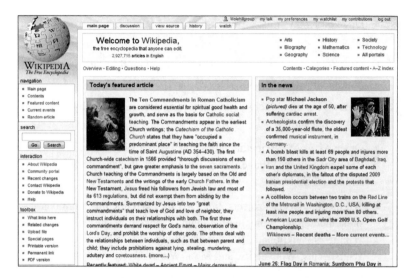

**FIGURE 2.2**   Wikipedia's English-language main page.

▶ At the top of the page, tabs to discuss and view the history and source code for this main page

▶ A navigation pane down the left side of the page

▶ Near the top of the page, a list of major topic portals (Arts, Biography, and so on); click any topic link to view a page devoted to that category

▶ Just below these topic links, links to various indices and lists (Contents), major categories (Categories), Featured Content, and an A-Z Index of all available topics

▶ To the left of these links, links to an Overview of how to use Wikipedia; an Editing tutorial on how to contribute and edit Wikipedia articles; a guide to how to ask Questions about the Wikipedia site; and to Wikipedia's Help system

▶ Today's Featured Article, an article singled out for viewing by the Wikipedia staff

▶ In the News, a list of articles related to current events

- ▶ Did You Know, a list of interesting facts culled from the newest articles

- ▶ On This Day, a list of events that happened on this date in the past

- ▶ Today's Featured Picture, an interesting picture picked by the Wikipedia staff

- ▶ Other Areas of Wikipedia, quick links to the Help Desk, Reference Desk, Village Pump, Community Portal, Site News, and Local Embassy

- ▶ Wikipedia's Sister Projects, links to other Wikimedia Commons sites, including Commons (the main organization site), Wikinews, Wiktionary, Wikiquote, Wikibooks, Wikisource, Wikispecies, Wikiversity, and Meta-Wiki

- ▶ Wikipedia Languages, links to the Wikipedia site in other languages

---

CAUTION: **Discussion**
The Discussion tab at the top of Wikipedia's main page does not lead to a general discussion about Wikipedia, or of any topics on this page. Instead, it leads to a specialized discussion about the makeup of the main page.

---

# Navigating Wikipedia

You do most of your navigation of the Wikipedia site using the navigation pane found on the left side of all pages on the site. From top to bottom, here's what you find in the navigation pane:

- ▶ A Navigation panel, with links to the Main Page, Contents, Featured Content, Current Events, and a Random Article

- ▶ A Search box, for searching the Wikipedia site

▶ An Interaction panel for interacting with the Wikipedia site, with links to About Wikipedia, Community Portal, Recent Changes, Contact Wikipedia, Donate to Wikipedia, and Help

▶ Toolbox, with tools appropriate to the current page, including What Links Here (links to the current page), Related Changes (changes in pages linked to this page), Upload File (for uploading images and other media files), Special Pages (a list of all special pages on the site), Printable Version (displays a version of the page suitable for printing), and Permanent Link (displays the URL to link to this page)

▶ Languages, with links to all major language versions of Wikipedia

This navigation pane is present on all pages on the Wikipedia site, including all article pages. This is particularly important when you search for information because this pane contains the search box you use for that task.

> NOTE: **Searching**
> Learn how to use Wikipedia's search box in Lesson 3, "Searching for Information."

# Featured Content

When you click the Featured Content link in the Wikipedia navigation pane, you're taken to a page full of items specially selected by the Wikipedia staff. As stated on this page, this content purports to represent "the best that Wikipedia has to offer"; all of this featured content goes through a review process before it's selected to appear on this page.

The Featured Content portal, shown in Figure 2.3, contains the following content:

**FIGURE 2.3**    The Featured Content portal.

- ▶ Featured Article
- ▶ Featured List
- ▶ Featured Picture
- ▶ Featured Sound
- ▶ Featured Portal
- ▶ Featured Topic

Each piece of featured content appears in its own box on the page. Below the featured content is a list of New Featured Content of all types.

# Topic Portals

The Featured Content page is just one of several *portal* pages. A Wikipedia portal is essentially a main page for a given topic. A portal page collects articles, lists, and other content related to the topic, presenting these links in a logical and organized fashion.

For example, Figure 2.4 shows the Dinosaur portal. This page includes an introduction, a selected article and picture, a Did You Know? interesting fact, a list of related topics, a list of related tasks, a list of topics within the category, and a list of related content.

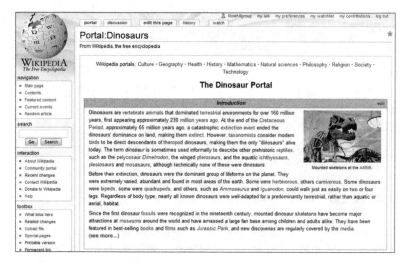

**FIGURE 2.4** The Dinosaur portal.

There are more than 500 portals on the Wikipedia site. To view a list of portals, click the All Portals link at the top of the Wikipedia main page.

# Browsing by Category

Although most users search Wikipedia for the information that they seek, you can also browse for specific articles by category. When you click the Categories link on the main page, you see the Categorical Index portal, shown in Figure 2.5.

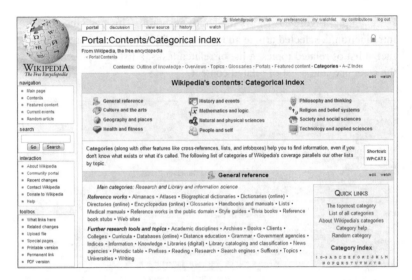

**FIGURE 2.5**    Wikipedia's Categorical Index portal.

This page is divided into a dozen major categories: General Reference, Culture and the Arts, Geography and Places, Health and Fitness, History and Events, Mathematics and Logic, Natural and Physical Sciences, People and Self, Philosophy and Thinking, Religion and Belief Systems, Society and Social Sciences, and Technology and Applied Sciences.

Within each of these major categories is a listing of subcategories. Click a subcategory link to view a page of further subcategories, which link to even more subcategories; keep clicking until you see a list of available pages, and then click to read an individual article.

# Using the A-to-Z Index

If you know the specific topic you want, you can skip the category browsing and go directly to the appropriate article on the Wikipedia site. To this end, Wikipedia includes an A-to-Z list of all articles. To view this list, click the A-Z Index at the top of the main page. This displays a list of letters (actually, first and second letter combinations); click a letter to view a list of articles starting with that letter, and then click an article link to read the article.

# Timelines

Some topics are easier understood by examining a timeline of key events. For example, Figure 2.6 shows a timeline of French history; key events are actually links to other Wikipedia articles.

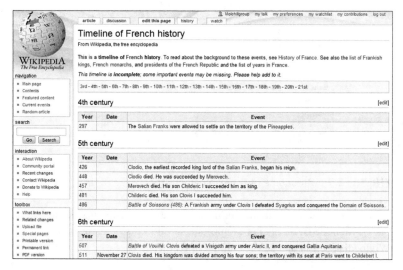

**FIGURE 2.6**    A timeline of French history.

To view a list of all available timelines, click the Contents link on the main page; when the Contents portal appears, scroll to the Timelines section and select List of Timelines.

# Outlines

Another way to get a handle on complex topics is to view an outline of that topic. Wikipedia puts together outlines for many major topics, like the one shown in Figure 2.7. An outline consists of a handful of major headings, with links to related articles within each heading; in essence, each subhead in the outline is an article on the Wikipedia site.

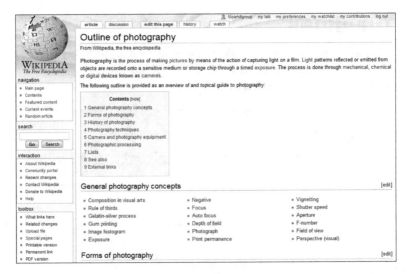

**FIGURE 2.7**    An outline of the photography topic.

To view a list of all available outlines, click the Contents link on the main page; when the Contents portal appears, scroll to the Overviews of Wikipedia section and select Outline of Knowledge.

> TIP: **Starting Point**
> A Wikipedia outline is a good starting point if you're researching or writing about a given topic.

# Glossaries

If you ever run across a word in a Wikipedia article and don't know what it means, you can look it up in one of the site's topic-oriented glossaries. Wikipedia includes more than a hundred different glossaries, for topics from alternative medicine to woodworking. (Figure 2.8 shows a typical glossary.)

**FIGURE 2.8**    A glossary of nautical terms.

---

PLAIN ENGLISH: **Glossary**

A list of specialized terms and their meanings.

---

To view a list of all available glossaries, click the Contents link on the main page; when the Contents portal appears, scroll to the Glossaries section and select either List of Glossaries or Category:Glossaries.

---

TIP: **Wikipedia Glossary**

Wikipedia even contains a glossary of Wikipedia-related terms, located at en.wikipedia.org/wiki/Wikipedia:Glossary.

---

# Wikipedia in Different Languages

As previously noted in this lesson, Wikipedia offers articles written in more than 250 different languages. You can access the different-language versions of Wikipedia directly from the www.wikipedia.org home page.

The top ten languages are arranged around the globe graphic at the top of this home page. These languages include English (more than 2.9 million articles), German (more than 900,000 articles), French (more than 800,000 articles), Polish (more than 600,000 articles), Japanese (close to 600,000 articles), Italian (more than 580,000 articles), Dutch (more than 540,000 articles), Spanish (more than 480,000 articles), Portuguese (more than 480,000 articles), and Russian (just over 400,000 articles). Below the globe are lists of other languages for which articles are available, organized by number of articles.

To view all the articles written in a given language, click that language link on the Wikipedia home page. This opens a main page for that language, like the one shown in Figure 2.9. Each language page has its own unique URL; for example, Wikipedia Japan is ja.wikipedia.org, whereas Wikipedia Netherlands (Dutch) is nl.wikipedia.org.

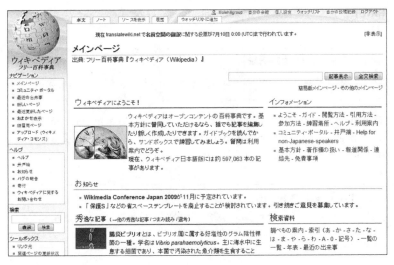

**FIGURE 2.9**    The main page for Wikipedia Japan.

CAUTION: **Size**

Some languages have only a few hundred articles available.

# Summary

In this lesson, you learned how to navigate the Wikipedia site. In the next lesson, you learn to search the site for specific information.

# LESSON 3

# Searching for Information

*In this lesson, you learn how to find specific articles on the Wikipedia site.*

## Conducting a Search

Searching for information on Wikipedia is similar to using a traditional search engine. You can use the search box on the www.wikipedia.org home page or the one in the navigation pane that appears on every Wikipedia page.

To search Wikipedia, enter your query into any one of these search boxes. Your query should consist of one or more keywords related to the topic in which you're interested; the more precise you can describe what you're searching for, the better the results will be.

PLAIN ENGLISH: **Keyword**
A word or phrase in a search query that describes what is being searched for.

When you use the home page search box, shown in Figure 3.1, you must select the language you want from the adjacent list; then click the right-arrow "go" button. When you use the navigation pane search box, shown in Figure 3.2, Wikipedia already knows which language you're using.

**FIGURE 3.1**    The search box on the Wikipedia home page.

**FIGURE 3.2**    The search box in the Wikipedia navigation pane.

However, the navigation pane search box has two buttons you can click. When you click the Go button, Wikipedia displays the article that it thinks is the best match for your query. When you click the Search button, Wikipedia displays a traditional page of search results, listing multiple articles that might match your query.

# Viewing Search Results

What happens after you initiate a Wikipedia search depends on which button you click: Search or Go.

## Searching from Search

Figure 3.3 displays a typical list of search results that appears when you click the Search button. As you can see, this is a rather traditional list of search results, displaying links to articles that feature or link to your keywords. Click any link to view the article in full.

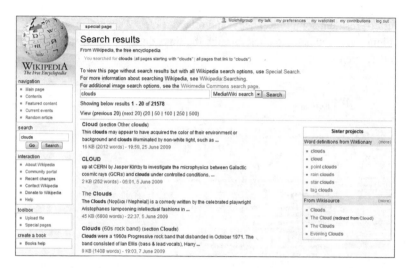

**FIGURE 3.3**  A search results page that results from clicking the Search button.

CAUTION: **Ambiguity**

If your query is too vague, Wikipedia's search results might include a link to a disambiguation page—discussed next.

This search results page sometimes includes a box on the right side of the page with links to so-called sister projects. For example, you might see links to definitions of a query keyword in the Wiktionary, quotes about the subject in Wikiquotes, or books about the topic in Wikibooks or Wikisource. Click a link to see what's available.

# Searching from Go

Even if you click the Go button, you still might see a list of articles—especially if the query is sufficiently vague. For example, if you search for **robert kennedy** and click the Go button, Wikipedia displays the article on Robert F. Kennedy. If, instead, you search only for **kennedy** and click the Go button Wikipedia, a *disambiguation* page appears, with sections for people, places, transportation, schools and colleges, places named after President John F. Kennedy, and other articles. As you can see in Figure 3.4, you need to click through the links on this page to get to the article you want.

**FIGURE 3.4**   A typical disambiguation page.

---

PLAIN ENGLISH: **Disambiguation**

The process of clarifying an ambiguity. In Wikipedia, a disambiguation page displays possible results from an ambiguous search.

---

# Conducting an Advanced Search

By default, Wikipedia displays a list of articles that match your search query. But other types of content are on the Wikimedia Commons family of sites, and you can choose to redirect your query to different types of content.

You do this by scrolling to the bottom of the search results page until you see the Advanced Search box, shown in Figure 3.5. Check the type of content you want to search; then click the Advanced Search button.

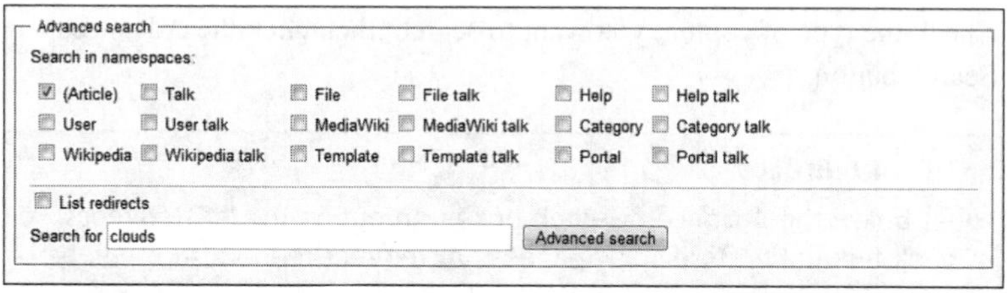

**FIGURE 3.5**   Performing an advanced search.

What types of content can you search? Here's the list:

▶ Article (default search)

▶ Talk (discussions about articles)

▶ Category (topic categories on the site)

▶ Category talk (discussions about categories)

▶ Portal (main topic pages)

▶ Portal talk (discussions about portal pages)

▶ File (pictures, sounds, and other media files)

▶ File talk (discussions about files)

▶ User (registered Wikipedia users)

▶ User talk (discussions about users)

▶ Wikipedia (comments from Wikipedia editors)

▶ Wikipedia talk (discussions about editorial comments)

▶ Help (Wikipedia's Help system)

▶ Help talk (discussions about the Help system)

▶ Template (the template pages used to create new articles)

▶ Template talk (discussions about templates)

▶ MediaWiki (the application that drives Wikipedia)

▶ MediaWiki talk (discussions about the MediaWiki engine)

Check the type of content you want to search; then click the Advanced Search button.

> **NOTE: Redirects**
> Just below the Advanced Search box is an option to List Redirects. Check this option to display pages that redirect readers to other, typically related, articles on the Wikipedia site.

# Searching Other Sites

Wikipedia also lets you route your search to other search engines on the Web. At the top of the search results page is a search box with a pull-down list, as shown in Figure 3.6. Pull down this list to display other search options: MediaWiki, Google, Yahoo, Bing, Wikiwx, and Exalead. Make your selection and then click the Search button; you now see a list of search results from the site you selected.

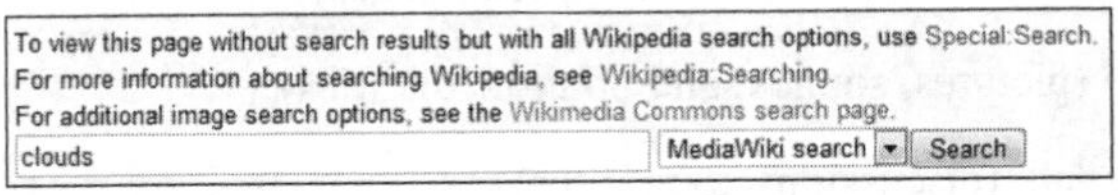

**FIGURE 3.6**  Expand your search to other websites.

# Fine-Tuning Your Search

Whether you use the Go or the Search button, you can do things within your query to achieve better search results. Here are some tips you can use to fine-tune your Wikipedia queries.

## Wildcards and Fuzzy Queries

It's not always easy to be sure of the spelling of a word, or which tense of a word is used in the article's title. To that end, Wikipedia allows the use of *wildcards* to "stand in" for additional characters in a keyword.

PLAIN ENGLISH: **Wildcard**

A single character (typically an asterisk) that matches any character or group of characters in a keyword, from its specific position in the keyword forward or backward.

The wildcard character used by Wikipedia is the asterisk: *. When you add an asterisk to a keyword, Wikipedia searches for all words that match the keyword up to the asterisk. For example, if you're not sure whether you want to search for automobile, automotive, or autos, enter **auto*** to return results for all three words (as well as automatic, autocratic, and any other word that starts with "auto").

You can add wildcards to the end or the front of a keyword. For example, if you want to search for all countries in Central Asia that end in the letters "stan," enter the query ***stan**.

Wikipedia also allows so-called *fuzzy queries*—searches for similar words. To initiate a fuzzy search, add a ~ to the end of the word. For example, if you enter the query **elderly~**, Wikipedia returns results for the words elderly, elder, eldership, elderon, Eldred, Elderoy (a town in Illinois), and even orderly.

# Exact Phrases

Normally, a multiple-word query searches for articles and topics that include all the words in the query, in any order. To search for an exact phrase, however, you must enclose the phrase in quotation marks.

For example, if you search for the Rev. Martin Luther King's famous speech, you should enter **"i have a dream"**, with quotation marks around the phrase. Similarly if you search for Monty Python, search for **"monty python"**.

# Boolean Searches

Another way to fine-tune your query is to use *Boolean operators*—short words that modify the logic of a query. Although Wikipedia does not use traditional Boolean searching (using the AND, OR, and NOT operators), it does support Boolean fulltext search. In this version of Boolean search, the + sign is used in place of the AND operator, and the – sign is used in place of the NOT operator.

Here's the way it works. If you want a match to contain *both* words in a query, put the + sign between the two words. So searching for **monty + python** returns articles about Monty Python or articles about pythons owned by guys named Monty, but *not* pages that include only one of the two words.

On the other hand, if you want a match to *exclude* the next word, put a – sign before the word to be excluded. So searching for **monty –python** return articles about guys named Monty but will *not* return pages about Monty Python.

> TIP: **+ Searches**
> When you create a + search, know that you're searching for both the words but *not necessarily in order*. If you want to search for both words in order, next to each other, you want to search for the exact phrase, which you do by putting the phrase in parentheses.

> PLAIN ENGLISH: **Boolean Logic**
> A form of algebra in which all values are reduced to either TRUE or FALSE. A *Boolean expression* results in a value of either TRUE or FALSE (if a page matches all conditions of a query, the result is TRUE) and contains *Boolean operators*, such as AND, OR, or NOT.

## Intitle Queries

By default, a Wikipedia query searches both article titles and article content. If you want to limit your search to titles only, use the **intitle:** operator. Just insert this operator in your query before the first keyword, like this: **intitle:query**. Don't insert a space between the operator and the keyword.

## Summary

In this lesson, you learned how to search the Wikipedia site. In the next lesson, you learn to read a Wikipedia article.

# LESSON 4

# Reading a Wikipedia Article

*In this lesson, you learn how to read a Wikipedia article.*

## Behind the Articles

A Wikipedia article is similar to an article in a traditional encyclopedia—but with links to other information on Wikipedia and across the Web. Of course, a Wikipedia article is also never finished; the site's users can continually edit and revise the article to reflect new events and discovered knowledge.

Naturally, the amount of information in any given article depends on the contributions of the users who helped to create the article. Some articles are embarrassingly brief, others are almost overwhelmingly comprehensive. The community strives for accuracy, of course, but can't dictate the actual content.

One interesting facet of Wikipedia articles is that they tend to change over time. This, again, is a factor of Wikipedia's collaborative nature. Users have the ability to edit the articles they read, so it's not unusual to see more (and more accurate) information added to articles over time. You, in fact, might be tempted to edit articles you encounter, especially if the article is on a topic that you know well.

> CAUTION: **Additional Citations Needed**
> If an article hasn't been thoroughly researched, you might see a note at the top of the page stating that the article "needs additional citations for verification." If you see this note, know that the article has not yet been verified and might contain incomplete or incorrect information.

So don't read an article and expect it to be the final word on a topic. That "final word" can change tomorrow or the next day—and hopefully become more complete and accurate as time goes by.

> NOTE: **Editing Articles**
>
> Learn more about editing Wikipedia articles in Lesson 9, "Editing an Existing Article."

# The Main Article

Because articles are written to an underlying template, all Wikipedia articles contain the same basic components. What's contained within an article, however, depends on the amount of information available.

Some shorter articles, like the one in Figure 4.1, are only a few paragraphs long. These articles have no need for summaries or tables of contents; what you get is the text itself and a list of footnoted references to the sources used within the article.

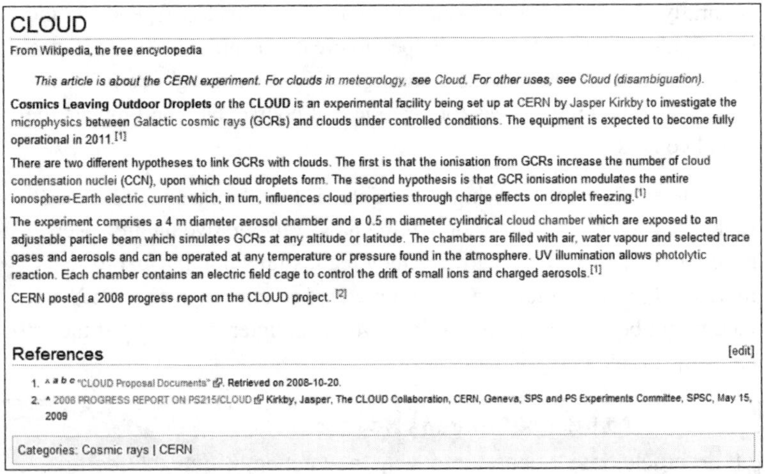

---

## CLOUD

From Wikipedia, the free encyclopedia

*This article is about the CERN experiment. For clouds in meteorology, see Cloud. For other uses, see Cloud (disambiguation).*

**Cosmics Leaving Outdoor Droplets** or the **CLOUD** is an experimental facility being set up at CERN by Jasper Kirkby to investigate the microphysics between Galactic cosmic rays (GCRs) and clouds under controlled conditions. The equipment is expected to become fully operational in 2011.[1]

There are two different hypotheses to link GCRs with clouds. The first is that the ionisation from GCRs increase the number of cloud condensation nuclei (CCN), upon which cloud droplets form. The second hypothesis is that GCR ionisation modulates the entire ionosphere-Earth electric current which, in turn, influences cloud properties through charge effects on droplet freezing.[1]

The experiment comprises a 4 m diameter aerosol chamber and a 0.5 m diameter cylindrical cloud chamber which are exposed to an adjustable particle beam which simulates GCRs at any altitude or latitude. The chambers are filled with air, water vapour and selected trace gases and aerosols and can be operated at any temperature or pressure found in the atmosphere. UV illumination allows photolytic reaction. Each chamber contains an electric field cage to control the drift of small ions and charged aerosols.[1]

CERN posted a 2008 progress report on the CLOUD project.[2]

### References                                                                    [edit]

  1. ^ a b c "CLOUD Proposal Documents" ᵠ. Retrieved on 2008-10-20.
  2. ^ 2008 PROGRESS REPORT ON PS215/CLOUD ᵠ Kirkby, Jasper, The CLOUD Collaboration, CERN, Geneva, SPS and PS Experiments Committee, SPSC, May 15, 2009

Categories: Cosmic rays | CERN

---

**FIGURE 4.1**   A short Wikipedia article.

Longer Wikipedia articles are organized into a summary and main sections. The summary is the first few paragraphs, just below the article's title, as shown in Figure 4.2. This is a general overview of the topic covered by the article; it covers in brief what the balance of the article covers in depth.

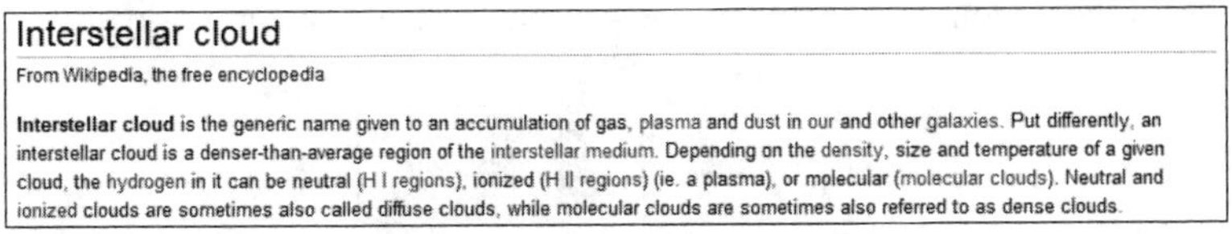

Interstellar cloud

From Wikipedia, the free encyclopedia

**Interstellar cloud** is the generic name given to an accumulation of gas, plasma and dust in our and other galaxies. Put differently, an interstellar cloud is a denser-than-average region of the interstellar medium. Depending on the density, size and temperature of a given cloud, the hydrogen in it can be neutral (H I regions), ionized (H II regions) (ie. a plasma), or molecular (molecular clouds). Neutral and ionized clouds are sometimes also called diffuse clouds, while molecular clouds are sometimes also referred to as dense clouds.

**FIGURE 4.2** The summary of a longer Wikipedia article.

Longer articles have a table of contents box, located beneath the summary, as shown in Figure 4.3. The table of contents also serves as an outline to the article's content; click any heading or subheading in the TOC to scroll directly to that section in the article.

**Contents** [hide]

1 Condensation
2 Classification of clouds
2.1 High clouds (Family A)
2.2 Middle clouds (Family B)
2.3 Low clouds (Family C)
2.4 Vertical clouds (Family D)
2.5 Other clouds
2.6 Cloud fields
3 Colors
4 Clouds and climate
4.1 Global brightening
4.2 Bacteria in clouds
5 Clouds on other planets
6 See also
7 Gallery
8 References
9 Bibliography
10 External links

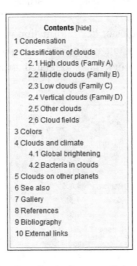

**FIGURE 4.3** The table of contents for an article.

The article itself starts just after the table of contents. Some articles are no more than a few sentences long; others contain multiple sections and require much scrolling of your web browser. Within the article, blue text indicates links to other articles within Wikipedia; click the text to jump to the related article.

Many articles contain photographs, drawings, maps, and other graphics in small boxes scattered throughout the main text. These boxes, like the one in Figure 4.4, illustrate key concepts from the text. Click the Enlarge button at the bottom-right corner of the graphic to view a larger version.

Clouds in sunlight from a low sun

**FIGURE 4.4**   A picture accompanying an article.

Other articles contain tables of key information within the main text. As you can see in Figure 4.5, this is a great way to present certain types of data; some tables even include links to related articles within the table itself.

| Element | Parts per million by mass |
|---|---|
| Hydrogen | 739,000 |
| Helium | 240,000 |
| Oxygen | 10,400 |
| Carbon | 4,600 |
| Neon | 1,340 |
| Iron | 1,090 |
| Nitrogen | 960 |
| Silicon | 650 |
| Magnesium | 580 |
| Sulfur | 440 |
| Potassium | 210 |
| Nickel | 100 |

**Figure 4.5**   Tabular information in a Wikipedia article.

In some articles, key information about the topic is presented in a sidebar to the right of the article. Figure 4.6 shows such an information sidebar, useful for grasping essential facts at a glance. For example, the information sidebar on the Nile river includes a picture of the river, the origin of the river's name, a list of countries through which the river flows, the location and elevation of the river, and the river's length (in kilometers and miles).

**FIGURE 4.6**    An article's information sidebar—key facts at a glance.

# Finding Additional Information

If you want to expand your research, scroll to the bottom of the article to the See Also section. This section contains a list of links to related Wikipedia articles; click any link to read the referenced article.

Scroll further down the page and you find the External Links section. This section contains links to other websites that might be of interest; click any link to go to the referenced site.

---

NOTE: **More Information**

Learn more about the See Also and External Links sections in Lesson 6, "Going Beyond an Article."

---

At the bottom of the article is a list of Wikipedia categories that contain this topic. Some articles also include one or more lists of related topics; for example, the Nile article containslinks to Ancient Egypt and Rivers of Uganda topics.

# Footnotes and References

Wondering where the information within an article was sourced from? Most key facts are footnoted within the main text; the footnote appears as a blue hyperlinked number in parentheses, like the one in Figure 4.7. Click a footnote link, and you're taken to the Notes or References section at the bottom of the article page, where the source for that fact is listed. Most sources come from the Web; click the link for a source document, and you're taken to the original website.

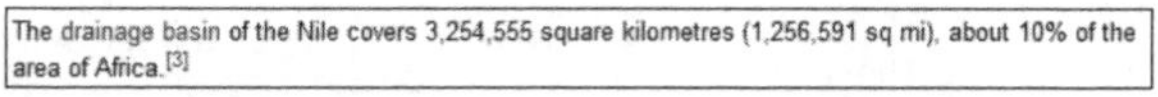

The drainage basin of the Nile covers 3,254,555 square kilometres (1,256,591 sq mi), about 10% of the area of Africa.[3]

**FIGURE 4.7**    A footnote that references the information source.

---

NOTE: **References**

Learn more about information sources in Lesson 5, "Verifying Information and Checking Resources."

---

# Discussions and History

Because Wikipedia is a collaborative encyclopedia, you can discuss any article you read with other users. Click the Discussion tab at the top of the page to view the Talk page for that article.

> NOTE: **Discussions**
>
> Learn more about article discussions in Lesson 8, "Discussing an Article."

In addition, all Wikipedia articles come with a history of revisions—that is, who changed what and when. To view the history for an article, click the History tab at the top of the page.

> NOTE: **History**
>
> Learn more about the History tab in Lesson 7, "Tracking Changes to an Article."

# Summary

In this lesson, you learned how to read a Wikipedia article. In the next lesson, you learn to verify the information contained in an article.

# LESSON 5

# Verifying Information and Checking References

*In this lesson, you learn how to verify the information you find in Wikipedia articles.*

## How Accurate Is an Article?

One of the primary issues some people have with Wikipedia concerns accuracy. Given that articles are written by other users, just how accurate is the information in an article?

Although the potential certainly exists for inaccurate information to be posted, Wikipedia maintains multiple safeguards to ensure the highest possible accuracy. Most of the safeguards revolve around *references*—the sources of information contained within an article.

Wikipedia is guided by what it calls the *five pillars*; these are general guidelines that define the type of content allowed on the site. The first pillar is the one that most affects the accuracy of the content; it is reproduced in full here:

**Wikipedia is an encyclopedia** incorporating elements of general and specialized encyclopedias, almanacs, and gazetteers. All articles must strive for verifiable accuracy: unreferenced material may be removed, so please provide references. Wikipedia is not the place to insert personal opinions, experiences, or arguments. Original ideas, interpretations, or research cannot be verified, and are thus inappropriate. Wikipedia is not a soapbox; an advertising platform; a vanity press; an experiment in anarchy or democracy; an indiscriminate collection of information; or a web directory. It is not a newspaper or a collection of source documents; these kinds of content should be contributed to the Wikimedia sister projects.

As you can see, this first pillar states explicitly the goal of "verifiable accuracy." This means that facts within an article must reference the sources of those facts. Articles without sufficient reference might be removed from the site.

Information references are thus key to ensuring the accuracy of any given article on the Wikipedia site. Readers might challenge an article with insufficient references or wholly unsourced material. An article without sufficient references might then be tagged as needing additional verification—or might simply be removed from the site.

NOTE: **Valid Research**
Learn more about verifying Wikipedia content in Lesson 19, "Using Wikipedia for Research and School Papers."

# Referencing Sources

When you read an article, key information within the text is often followed by a footnote. This footnote indicates that the information in the preceding sentence or sentences is referenced from another source.

To view the source of that information, click the footnote—which is actually a link to that source in the References section of the article. As you can see in Figure 5.1, the References section includes a list of citations for various information within the article. Each citation is to a book, magazine article, academic paper, or website; most sources are available on the Web and are linked from the References list. To view the original source material, simply click the citation link in the References list.

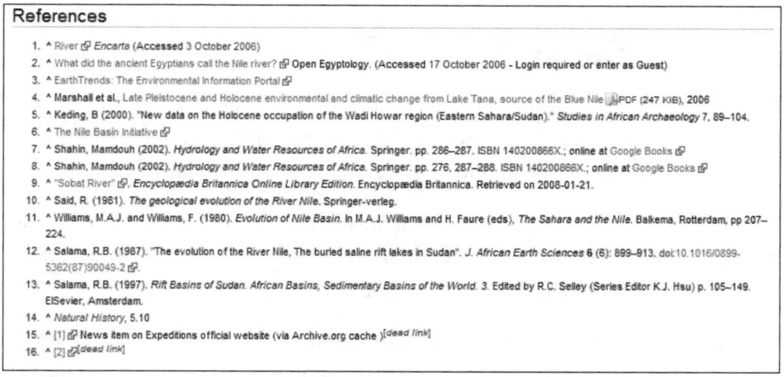

References

1. ^ River *Encarta* (Accessed 3 October 2006)
2. ^ What did the ancient Egyptians call the Nile river? Open Egyptology. (Accessed 17 October 2006 - Login required or enter as Guest)
3. ^ EarthTrends: The Environmental Information Portal
4. ^ Marshall et al., Late Pleistocene and Holocene environmental and climatic change from Lake Tana, source of the Blue Nile PDF (247 KiB), 2006
5. ^ Keding, B (2000). "New data on the Holocene occupation of the Wadi Howar region (Eastern Sahara/Sudan)." *Studies in African Archaeology* 7, 89–104.
6. ^ The Nile Basin Initiative
7. ^ Shahin, Mamdouh (2002). *Hydrology and Water Resources of Africa*. Springer. pp. 286–287. ISBN 140200866X.; online at Google Books
8. ^ Shahin, Mamdouh (2002). *Hydrology and Water Resources of Africa*. Springer. pp. 276, 287–288. ISBN 140200866X.; online at Google Books
9. ^ "Sobat River". *Encyclopædia Britannica Online Library Edition*. Encyclopædia Britannica. Retrieved on 2008-01-21.
10. ^ Said, R. (1981). *The geological evolution of the River Nile*. Springer-verleg.
11. ^ Williams, M.A.J. and Williams, F. (1980). *Evolution of Nile Basin*. In M.A.J. Williams and H. Faure (eds), *The Sahara and the Nile*. Balkema, Rotterdam, pp 207–224.
12. ^ Salama, R.B. (1987). "The evolution of the River Nile, The buried saline rift lakes in Sudan". *J. African Earth Sciences* **6** (6): 899–913. doi:10.1016/0899-5362(87)90049-2.
13. ^ Salama, R.B. (1997). *Rift Basins of Sudan. African Basins, Sedimentary Basins of the World. 3*. Edited by R.C. Selley (Series Editor K.J. Hsu) p. 105–149. ElSevier, Amsterdam.
14. ^ *Natural History*, 5.10
15. ^ [1] News item on Expeditions official website (via Archive.org cache )[dead link]
16. ^ [2] [dead link]

**FIGURE 5.1** Citations in an article's References section.

> PLAIN ENGLISH: **Citation**
>
> A short note recognizing the source of a piece of information or quotation.

Citation format differs according to the type of source referenced and the dictates of specific fields of interest. In general, however, you can find some or all of the following information:

- The name of the document's author(s)
- The year or date of publication
- The title of the article
- The title of the book or publication, or the name of the website
- The page numbers from the original book or publication
- The name of the publisher

If the source information is available on the Internet, the citation includes a link to the source, often accompanied by a retrieval date. Obviously, not all forms of information are available online; in particular, don't expect links to books or academic journals.

# Verifying Information

Citations are important to verify the facts within an article. With the source cited, other users and editors can quickly and easily check where the information came from and thus the accuracy of that information.

In addition, citations help to guard against plagiarism. Because it's easy to compare the content of a Wikipedia article with the source material, blatant copying can be easily identified and flagged.

Finally, citations help users find additional information on a topic. When key facts are derived from source material, you can often find other useful information by referring back to the source.

Reading the source material is as easy as clicking on the source name within a citation, if available; this displays the original document within your web browser. For sources not online, you need to visit your local library.

CAUTION: **Source Documents**
Source documents referenced in a citation are not part of the Wikipedia site and must be treated separately.

Note, however, that the aim of Wikipedia, in its own words, is "verifiability, not truth." Wikipedia's goal is to provide the tools necessary for users to verify the information they find but not necessarily to verify that information as being truthful. So it's enough for an article to link to an external source, even if that external source is itself inaccurate.

In the eyes of the Wikipedia staff, it's not their role to determine what is or isn't true. Although this position is commendable when presenting both sides of controversial issues, it can be a bit of a cop out when presenting what should be clearly factual information. So it's left to you, the reader, to not just verify the source of key information, but also to verify the accuracy of the information presented at the source.

> NOTE: **Challenging Accuracy**
> If you come across an article that you believe contains inaccurate information, you can challenge the article or correct it yourself. Learn more in Lesson 9, "Editing an Existing Article."

# Summary

In this lesson, you learned how to verify the accuracy of an article. In the next lesson, you learn to find more information beyond that presented in an article.

# LESSON 6

# Going Beyond an Article

*In this lesson, you learn how to find additional information beyond that presented in a single article.*

## Reading Related Articles

In many ways, a Wikipedia article is just the starting point for your informational journey. Although many articles can tell you all you want to know about a topic, there is often more information to be had—both on and off the Wikipedia site.

The first place to look for more information is on Wikipedia itself. Several places within any given article link to additional articles that might be of interest.

One good place to find additional information is within the text of the article. Any blue text you find is actually a link to other articles on the Wikipedia site. So, for example, if you read the article on the Grand Canyon and see the words "Colorado River" in blue, clicking that phrase displays an article about the Colorado River. This takes full advantage of the Web's hyperlinked nature; just click to find out more about any highlighted word or phrase.

You can find other relevant articles in the See Also section at the bottom of the article page. As you can see in Figure 6.1, this section links to a variety of related articles. In the case of the Grand Canyon article, there are See Also links to articles on the Grand Canyon National Park, Arizona's Jacob Lake, the 1956 Grand Canyon mid-air collision, and more. Click any link to view the full article.

**FIGURE 6.1** The See Also section contains links to related Wikipedia articles.

In some articles, even more links are available at the bottom of the page, where related topics are listed. As you can see in Figure 6.2, these sections include links to articles about these topics; click the Show link to expand the section to display all available links. For example, the Grand Canyon article includes a list of articles related to the State of Arizona and articles related to the Colorado River System.

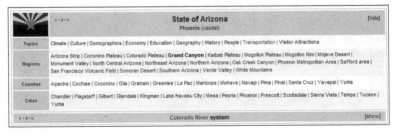

**FIGURE 6.2** View articles on related topics at the bottom of most article pages.

Finally, many articles present a Categories list at the bottom of the page, as shown in Figure 6.3. This is a list of categories that encompass the topic of the current article. Click a category to view a full list of subcategories articles within the category, like the one shown in Figure 6.4. You can explore the category from there.

> Categories: Canyons and gorges of Arizona | Grand Canyon | Southwestern United States | Colorado Plateau | Physiographic sections | Colorado River

**FIGURE 6.3** A list of categories related to the current article.

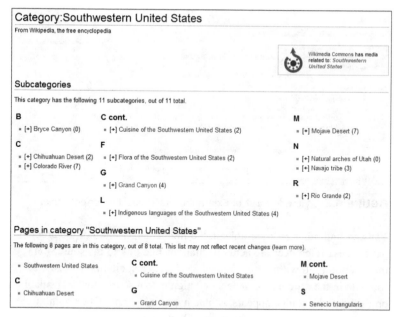

**FIGURE 6.4**    Viewing a Wikipedia category page.

---

TIP: **A Better Understanding**

Reading these related articles provides a bigger picture view of the original topic. Sometimes it's good to read "around the edges" of a topic in this fashion; it broadens your understanding of the topic at hand.

---

# Viewing Related Web Pages

Wikipedia is a great source of information, but it's not the only source of information. Remember, Wikipedia gets its facts from outside sources—which can often be accessed to provide more information about the topic.

The first place to look for outside information is near the bottom of most article pages, in the External Links section. As you can see in Figure 6.5, this section includes links to web pages about the topic at hand. Click a link to view the external page.

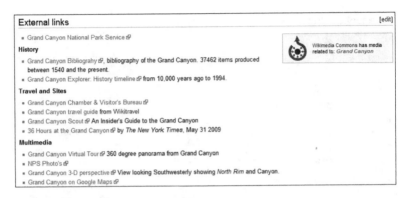

**FIGURE 6.5**    Viewing a list of External Links about the current topic.

You can find other external links in the References section of the article page. These references are actually citations that link to the sources of information used within the Wikipedia article; each citation is linked to a footnote in the article text. When a citation is to a source that is available on the web, the source appears as blue hyperlinked text. Click a link to view the source material on its original Web page.

# Summary

In this lesson, you learned how to find additional information related to a given article. In the next lesson, you learn to track the changes made over time to an article.

# LESSON 7

# Tracking Changes to an Article

*In this lesson, you learn how to view an article's history and track revisions to the article.*

## Viewing an Article's History

Because Wikipedia is a user-edited encyclopedia, any article can be edited by any number of users. For some articles, this creates a long history of revisions, from the article's original text through all its edits to the article in its current state.

It's sometimes useful to peruse an article's history, especially with topics that reference current events and unfolding situations. You can see how the known facts of a topic have changed over time, get a handle on prevailing opinion, and even track the depth of information available. In this fashion, it's often useful (and sometimes fun) to compare one version of an article with another.

For this reason, Wikipedia keeps a history of every article on its site. This history consists of all the old versions of the article, along with a record of the date and time of every edit—and who made those edits.

> NOTE: **History**
> An article's history is alternatively called a page history, edit history, or revision history.

# Examining the History Tab

To view the history of an article, click the History tab at the top of the article's page. As you can see in Figure 7.1, the History page consists of the following sections:

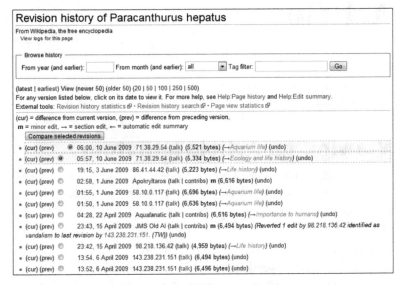

**FIGURE 7.1**    The History page of a Wikipedia article.

- ▶ A Browse History section that lets you filter the history results

- ▶ Links to external tools to view revision and page view statistics, and to search the revision history

- ▶ A Compare Selected Revisions button

- ▶ A list of the 50 most recent revisions made to this article

- ▶ At the bottom of the page, links to view older revisions

The revisions to an article are listed in reverse chronological order—that is, the latest revisions are at the top. The history page lists only the 50 most recent revisions; you need to click backward to view older edits.

To view a particular version of the article, click the date of that revision in the list. This displays the page as it existed on that date, with a note at the top of the page detailing the revision, as shown in Figure 7.2.

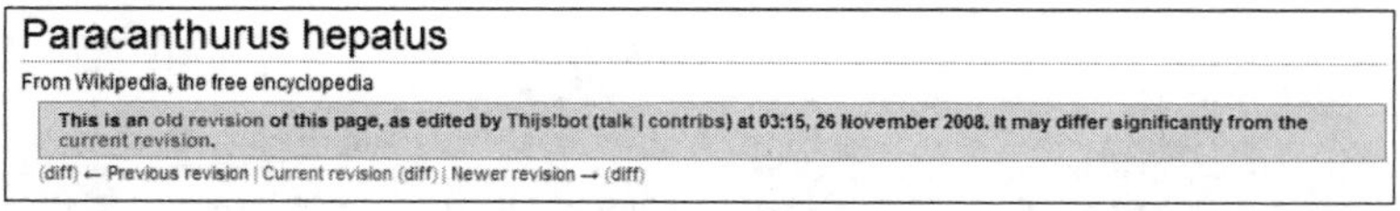

**Paracanthurus hepatus**

From Wikipedia, the free encyclopedia

This is an old revision of this page, as edited by Thijs!bot (talk | contribs) at 03:15, 26 November 2008. It may differ significantly from the current revision.

(diff) ← Previous revision | Current revision (diff) | Newer revision → (diff)

**FIGURE 7.2** Viewing an older version of an article.

# Comparing Revisions

You can compare different versions of an article in several ways. These include the following:

▶ To compare a specific revision with the current version, click the Cur link next to that revision.

▶ To compare a specific revision with the revision previous to that one, click the Prev link next to the first version.

▶ To compare any two versions, check the left-column radio button of the older version and the right-column radio button of the newer version; then click the Compare Selected Revisions button.

A revision comparison looks like that in Figure 7.3. Anything that's changed between versions is displayed side-by-side, with the newest version on the right. Changes are listed newest to oldest. A change might be minor (changing the formatting of a word or paragraph) or major (adding completely new material). Whatever the changes, they're easily visible in this side-by-side comparison.

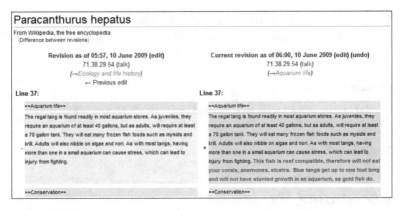

**FIGURE 7.3**    Comparing two different versions of an article.

# Filtering the Revision History

At the top of the History tab is a Browse History section, shown in Figure 7.4, which lets you filter the revisions displayed. This is useful when there are lots of changes to an article over time.

**FIGURE 7.4**    Use the Browse History section to filter the revision results.

You can filter the revisions in the following ways:

▶ **From year (and earlier):** Displays revisions dating to a specific year

▶ **From month (and earlier):** Displays revisions dating to a specific month within the past year

▶ **Tag filter:** Displays only those revisions that contain the specified keywords

Make your choices and then click the Go button.

# Searching an Article's History

You can also search an article's history for specific revisions. You use the WikiBlame tool for doing this, as follows:

1. From the History page, click the Revision History Search link just below the Browse History section.

2. When the WikiBlame page appears, as shown in Figure 7.5, enter the text you're searching for into the Search For box.

3. If you want to limit the search by date, make the appropriate changes to the Start Date field.

4. Click the Start button.

**FIGURE 7.5**   Using WikiBlame to search for specific revisions.

WikiBlame now displays a list of revisions that contain what you're looking for, organized by date (latest first). Click a date to view that particular version of the article.

---

TIP: **Linking**

There are times where you might want to link to a specific version of an article, which effectively acts as a snapshot in time. To link to an older revision, simply display the specific revision page and then copy that page's URL.

# Keeping Track of New Changes

Because Wikipedia articles are in constant development, you might want to be notified if and when a specific article changes. Wikipedia offers several ways to keep in touch with new edits.

## Viewing the Watch List

One way to keep track of changes to an article is to subscribe to that article's *watch list*. You can watch any number of pages and thus generate a list of changes to those pages.

> NOTE: **Log In**
>
> To use the watch list feature, you must be a registered user who is signed into the Wikipedia site. Registering is free and is done by clicking the Log In/Create Account link at the top of the Wikipedia main page.

To watch a page (and its associate discussion page) for changes, simply click the Watch tab at the top of the article's page. To stop watching an article, click the Unwatch tab.

To view articles on your watch list, click the My Watchlist link at the top of any Wikipedia page. This displays a list of all revisions to all pages you're watching, as shown in Figure 7.6. Revisions are listed in reverse chronological order, with all watched articles lumped in together.

My watchlist

From Wikipedia, the free encyclopedia
(for Molehillgroup)
Display watched changes | View and edit watchlist | Edit raw watchlist

Watchlist options

You have 3 pages on your watchlist (excluding talk pages).

Below are the last 4 changes, as of 22:19, 26 June 2009.
Show last 1 | 2 | 6 | 12 hours 1 | 3 | 7 days all
Hide minor edits | Hide bots | Hide anonymous users | Hide logged-in users | Hide my edits

Namespace: all ▼ ☐ Invert selection Go

**26 June 2009**

- (diff) (hist) . . **m** Batman; 08:33 . . (-31) . . Ckatz (talk | contribs) *(Reverted edits by 195.194.21.186 (talk) to last version by Gogo Dodo)*
- (diff) (hist) . . **m** Talk:Iran; 07:13 . . (+910) . . SoSaysChappy (talk | contribs) *(Reverted edits by 75.70.178.130 to last revision by Michigan10 (HG))*
- (diff) (hist) . . **mb** Iran; 00:29 . . (+14) . . TXiKiBoT (talk | contribs) *(robot Adding: vec:Iran)*

**25 June 2009**

- (diff) (hist) . . Talk:Batman; 07:03 . . (+282) . . J Greb (talk | contribs) *(→Batman is NOT exclusively Bruce Wayne: C)*

**FIGURE 7.6**   Viewing recent revisions to articles on a watch list.

# Viewing History via RSS Feed

You can also subscribe to a news feed that lists the revisions for any article in the Wikipedia database. The feed can be in RSS or Atom format; you view the feed in your feed reader software of choice.

> PLAIN ENGLISH: **News Feed**
>
> A data format that notifies users of or provides users with frequently updated content from websites, newsgroups, and the like. The two most popular feed formats are RSS (Really Simple Syndication) and Atom.

To create a feed for a given article, follow these steps:

**1.** Navigate to the article you want to track.

**2.** Click the History tab.

**3.** Click either RSS or Atom in the Toolbox panel of the navigation pane.

**4.** When the RSS or Atom feed page for this article appears, copy the page's URL into your feed reader software or website.

Your feed reader will now be notified of any changes made to this article.

TIP: **Newsreaders**

Popular newsreader programs include FeedDemon (www.feedde-mon.com) and FeedReader (www.feedreader.com). In addition, several websites, such as Google Reader (www.google.com/reader), aggregate RSS and Atom feeds.

# Summary

In this lesson, you learned how to track changes to a Wikipedia article. In the next lesson, you learn to discuss an article with other Wikipedia users.

# LESSON 8

# Discussing an Article

*In this lesson, you learn how to discuss the content of an article.*

## Viewing a Talk Page

Given any given group of users editing the same article, some discussion of what should be included in the article is only natural. After all, not every expert agrees on what's important.

When you want to discuss the content of an article, use that article's *talk page*. You access the talk page for an article by clicking the Discussion tab at the top of the main article page.

> CAUTION: **Article Improvements**
>
> A talk page is not the place to discuss the topic per se, but rather to discuss the contents of the article. So, for example, you wouldn't use the Abortion talk page to debate the issue of abortion, only to discuss how the Abortion article could be improved.

As you can see in Figure 8.1, the top of the talk page contents what is called the *bannerspace*—discussion guidelines and policies, article achievements, related pages, and links to past discussions. These items are similar from talk page to talk page.

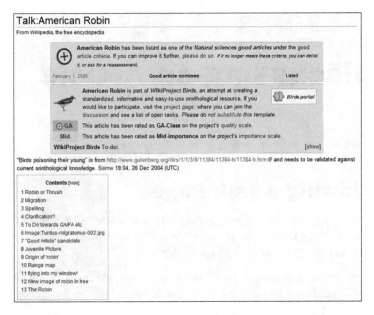

**FIGURE 8.1**    A talk page's bannerspace and TOC.

Beneath the bannerspace is the table of contents—a list of topics discussed on this page. In the TOC box, the most recent topics are listed last. Click any topic in the TOC to go directly to that section of the talk page.

Finally, we get to the list of discussion topics themselves. As you can see in Figure 8.2, each discussion topic is prefaced by a heading that details the topic. The initial comment on the topic is followed by any additional comments from other users. Each comment includes the name of the user who posted the comment, and the date and time of the comment.

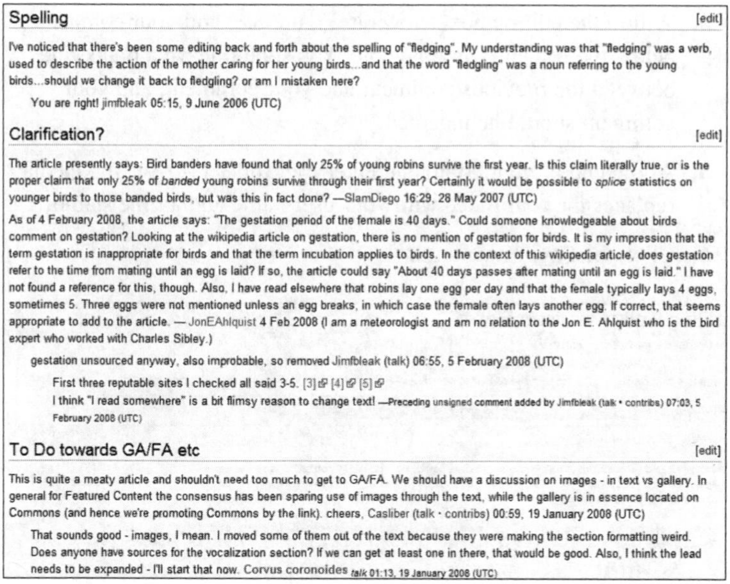

**FIGURE 8.2** Discussion topics on a talk page.

# Entering a Discussion

To enter a discussion on a talk page, you must edit the code behind the page. This is similar to editing a Wikipedia article and requires a bit of knowledge of the code language.

> NOTE: **Editing**
>
> Learn more about Wikipedia's code language in Lesson 9, "Editing an Existing Article."

## Responding to an Existing Topic

To respond to an existing topic on a talk page, follow these steps:

**1.** From the talk page, scroll to the topic to which you want to respond and click the Edit link.

2. Within the editing box, shown in Figure 8.3, add your comment below the last entry in this topic. You should leave a blank line between the previous comment and your comment, and your comment should be indented.

3. At the end of your comment, enter four tildes (~~~~). Wikipedia replaces the four tildes with your user name and a time stamp.

4. Click the Save Page button.

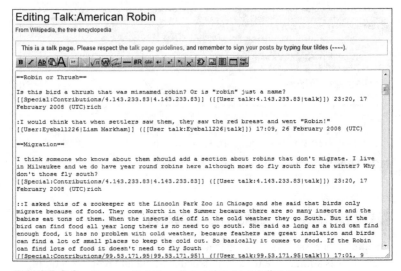

**FIGURE 8.3**   Responding to a discussion on a talk page.

# Entering a New Topic

You can also start new topics on a talk page. Follow these steps:

1. From the talk page, click the Edit This Page tab.

2. Within the editing box, scroll to the bottom of the box. (New topics are always added beneath all existing topics.)

3. Enter two equal signs (==), the title of your topic, and then two more equal signs. Your topic header should look like this: == **Topic** ==.

**4.** Enter the text for your discussion.

**5.** At the end of your comment, enter four tildes (~~~~). Wikipedia replaces the four tildes with your user name and a time stamp.

**6.** Click the Save Page button.

# What's Allowed—and What's Not

The purpose of a talk page is to enable editors to discuss proposed changes to an article. It is not a place to debate the underlying topics or to forward one's personal views.

So what can you discuss on a talk page? Because the goal is to improve the content of an article, you should discuss the article's content. You can discuss existing content that you feel is inaccurate or incomplete, or suggest new content that could be added. You can even discuss grammar and punctuation, as many users do.

Whatever you discuss, please do so courteously and concisely. Make your point and move on—and try not to offend other users while doing so.

You should make sure you read the entire talk page before you make a post; you don't want to make suggestions that have already been covered by other users. Make sure you comment on the page's content, not on the content's contributors. Keep it professional, not personal. (That means no personal attacks!) And remember, you're discussing the article, not debating the topic; there are other forums on the Web for those types of discussions.

# Summary

In this lesson, you learned how to post your comments to an article's talk page. In the next lesson, you learn to make edits to a Wikipedia article.

# LESSON 9

# Editing an Existing Article

*In this lesson, you learn how to revise articles on the Wikipedia site.*

## All About Editing

Wikipedia is a user-edited encyclopedia, which means that users like you can edit any article on the Wikipedia site. You can edit an article to correct bad punctuation or grammar, to fix factual errors, or to add more information.

Anyone can edit existing Wikipedia articles. You don't have to be approved by a board of authority, or pass muster with others on the site. All you need is to be a registered user (it's free) and take the time necessary to make the edits.

When you edit a page and click the Save Page button, the revised page is immediately available to other users. Your edits don't need to be vetted or approved in any way; you make the changes and everybody sees the changes. It's that easy and that fast.

Of course, "easy" is relevant. All Wikipedia pages are created with a special markup language, similar to the Web's HTML language. This Wiki Markup Language (also called Wikitext) uses special codes and characters to create specific types of formatting. For example, there's a special code that creates a section header, and another code that inserts an image into the article. You need to know the codes to edit any article.

PLAIN ENGLISH: **HTML**
Hypertext markup language, the code-based markup language used to create all pages on the Web.

Codes in hand, editing is as easy as clicking the Edit This Page tab and making your changes in the resulting text box. When you save your changes, the article is immediately revised.

# Making Your Edits

When you see a Wikipedia article that needs editing, follow these steps to make revisions:

**1.** From the article page, click the Edit This Page tab.

**2.** This displays a new page with a text box that contains the underlying code for the article, like the one shown in Figure 9.1. Make your edits to the text within this box.

**3.** Enter a summary of your changes into the Edit Summary box.

**4.** If this is a relatively minor edit (grammar, punctuation, formatting, and so forth), check the This is a Minor Edit box.

**5.** Click the Show Preview button to preview the article with your changes.

**6.** Click the Save Page button to save the revised article.

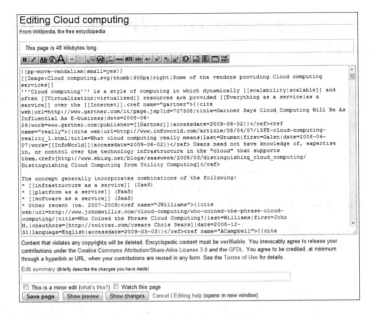

**FIGURE 9.1**  Editing an existing Wikipedia article.

Obviously, you need to insert the appropriate Wiki Markup Language codes into your text, where needed. You can also use the formatting toolbar above the editing box to automatically insert certain codes. For example, to italicize a piece of text, select the text in the editing box and then click the Italic Text button. There are buttons on the toolbar for basic formatting and for inserting links, pictures, tables, and other more sophisticated page elements.

---

TIP: **Be Bold—to a Point**

Although Wikipedia editors are encouraged to be bold with their revisions, you probably don't want to make major changes to an article without first getting the opinions of other users. You can do this by posting to the article's Talk page, as discussed in Lesson 8, "Discussing an Article."

---

# Understanding the Wiki Markup Language

You use the Wiki Markup Language to apply formatting to article text and to insert all manner of special elements, from tables to pictures to links to other articles and websites. A cursory knowledge of this language is necessary when editing articles on the Wikipedia site.

Most Wiki Markup Language commands are inserted between dual square brackets, like this: **[[command]]**. Some commands are enclosed between "on" and "off" angle brackets, similar to HTML tags, like this: **<command>text</command>**.

Although a comprehensive list of all available commands is beyond the scope of this lesson, here are the most common commands you're likely to use.

> NOTE: **Images**
> Learn more about Wiki Markup Language codes at en.wikipedia.org/wiki/Help:Editing.

## Article Links

When you want to link to other Wikipedia articles, use this code:

```
[[name of article]]
```

To use this code, you must know the proper name of the article to which you want to link. Just insert the name of the article between the dual square brackets. So, for example, if you want to link to the article on actor Paul Frees within a given sentence, the text would look like this:

```
Voice actor [[Paul Frees]] appeared in hundreds of radio and
television programs.
```

The resulting text looks like this, with the underlined text linking to the article on Paul Frees:

**Voice actor <u>Paul Frees</u> appeared in hundreds of radio and television programs.**

If you'd rather display different words within your text instead of the proper article name, use what Wikipedia calls a *renamed link*. The code for a renamed link looks like this:

```
[[name of article¦renamed text]]
```

Back to our Paul Frees example, if you wanted to refer to him as "Mr. Frees" in the text, the text would look like this:

```
In the 1960s, [[Paul Frees¦Mr. Frees]] provided several voices
for the Rocky and Bullwinkle cartoon show.
```

The resulting text looks like this, with the underlined text still linking to the Paul Frees article:

**In the 1960s, <u>Mr. Frees</u> provided several voices for the Rocky and Bullwinkle cartoon show.**

# Category Page Links

If, instead of linking to an article, you want to link to a topic category, you use a category page link. The code looks like this:

```
[[:Category:Category name]]
```

So, for example, if you want to link to the Mythology category, you'd enter this code:

```
[[:Category:Mythology]]
```

# External Links

You can also link from within a Wikipedia article to other pages on the Web. There are three ways to create this type of external link.

The first method is to create a bare link, one in which the entire URL is shown in the article text. The code for a bare external link looks like this:

```
http://www.website.com
```

That is, the link is just the text itself. For example, you might enter the following text:

```
The article originally appeared at http://www.cnn.com.
```

The results of that text look like this:

**The article originally appeared at http://www.cnn.com.**

> CAUTION: **Bare is Bad**
>
> Using bare links with raw URLs in your text is considered bad form in the Wikipedia community and should be avoided.

The second method is to create an unnamed link, one in which there is no text in the article associated with the link. This approach is used primarily for adding footnotes within the article body. The code looks like this:

```
[http://www.website.com]
```

This code creates a numbered footnote. For example, you might enter this text:

```
The original article appeared on CNN. [http://www.cnn.com]
```

The results of this text look like this:

**The original article appeared on CNN. [1]**

Finally, we come to the preferred method for creating external links, which lets you create named links. The code look like this:

```
[http://www.website.com linked-text]
```

For example, you might create this text and code:

```
The original report appeared on the [http://www.cnn.com CNN]
website.
```

The resulting text looks like this:

**The original report appeared on the CNN website.**

# Book Sources Link

Because many citations include references to books, Wikipedia lets you link to a special Book Sources page, as shown in Figure 9.2. Readers can then use this page to search for a specific book and even purchase it online.

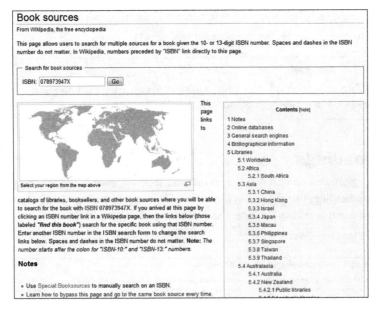

**FIGURE 9.2** Wikipedia's Book Sources page.

The code for linking to the Book Sources page is as follows:

```
ISBN 123456789
```

Obviously, replace the list of numbers with the nine-digit ISBN number for the book.

# Image and Sound Links

You can link to audio and image files that you previously uploaded to Wikipedia. To link a sound file, use this code:

```
[[media: filename.ext¦sound]
```

To link to an image file, use this code:

```
[[media:filename.jpg¦link text]]
```

To display an image on the page, insert this code:

```
[[Image:filename.jpg¦thumb]]
```

To insert an image with a caption beneath it, use this code:

```
[[Image:filename.jpg¦thumb¦caption text]]
```

> NOTE: **Images**
>
> Learn more about inserting images in Lesson 11, "Incorporating Pictures and Other Media in Your Article."

# Headings

Long articles are best divided into several sections, each section with its own heading, like the one in Figure 9.3. To insert a heading, simply enter two equal signs (==) on either side of the heading text, like this:

```
== Heading Text ==
```

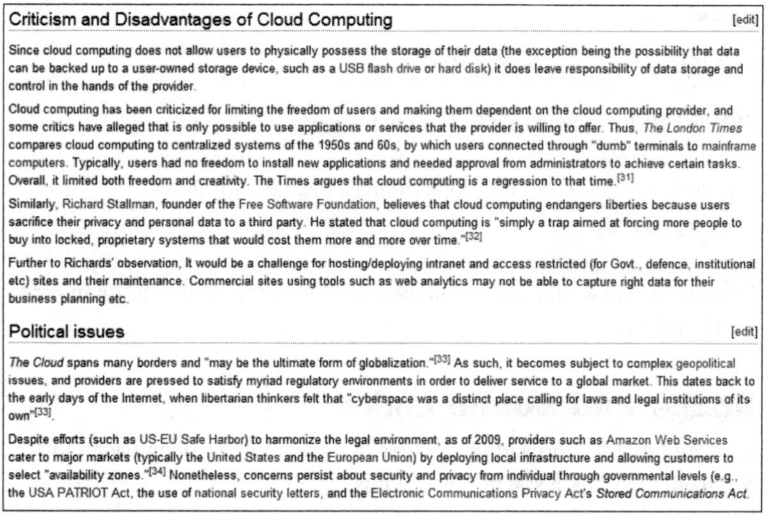

Criticism and Disadvantages of Cloud Computing [edit]

Since cloud computing does not allow users to physically possess the storage of their data (the exception being the possibility that data can be backed up to a user-owned storage device, such as a USB flash drive or hard disk) it does leave responsibility of data storage and control in the hands of the provider.

Cloud computing has been criticized for limiting the freedom of users and making them dependent on the cloud computing provider, and some critics have alleged that is only possible to use applications or services that the provider is willing to offer. Thus, *The London Times* compares cloud computing to centralized systems of the 1950s and 60s, by which users connected through "dumb" terminals to mainframe computers. Typically, users had no freedom to install new applications and needed approval from administrators to achieve certain tasks. Overall, it limited both freedom and creativity. The Times argues that cloud computing is a regression to that time.[31]

Similarly, Richard Stallman, founder of the Free Software Foundation, believes that cloud computing endangers liberties because users sacrifice their privacy and personal data to a third party. He stated that cloud computing is "simply a trap aimed at forcing more people to buy into locked, proprietary systems that would cost them more and more over time."[32]

Further to Richards' observation, It would be a challenge for hosting/deploying intranet and access restricted (for Govt., defence, institutional etc) sites and their maintenance. Commercial sites using tools such as web analytics may not be able to capture right data for their business planning etc.

Political issues [edit]

*The Cloud* spans many borders and "may be the ultimate form of globalization."[33] As such, it becomes subject to complex geopolitical issues, and providers are pressed to satisfy myriad regulatory environments in order to deliver service to a global market. This dates back to the early days of the Internet, when libertarian thinkers felt that "cyberspace was a distinct place calling for laws and legal institutions of its own"[33].

Despite efforts (such as US-EU Safe Harbor) to harmonize the legal environment, as of 2009, providers such as Amazon Web Services cater to major markets (typically the United States and the European Union) by deploying local infrastructure and allowing customers to select "availability zones."[34] Nonetheless, concerns persist about security and privacy from individual through governmental levels (e.g., the USA PATRIOT Act, the use of national security letters, and the Electronic Communications Privacy Act's *Stored Communications Act*.

**FIGURE 9.3** Headings in a Wikipedia article.

You can also insert subheadings beneath major headings. To do this, surround the subheading text with *three* equal signs (===), like this:

```
=== Subheading Text ===
```

You can even create lower-level subheadings beneath that, by using four or more equal signs around the subheading text.

# Citation References

Because key information you enter needs to be fully sourced, you have to insert footnotes into the text that reference citations in the article's References section. Fortunately, this text is somewhat automated via the **<ref>** code. Just enter this code (and the necessary citation details) at the end of appropriate article text, and Wikipedia automatically inserts a footnote into the text and places the citation in proper sequence in the References section.

The code itself is simple:

```
<ref>citation details</ref>
```

Naturally, you replace *citation details* with the actual details of the citation. Used in context, you might enter something like this:

```
Hal Blaine was the primary drummer behind the group of studio
musicians called the Wrecking Crew.<ref> Miller, Michael
(2005). ''The Complete Idiot's Guide to Playing Drums, 2nd
Edition''. Alpha Books. ISBN 1592574378</ref>
```

The resulting text looks like this:

**Hal Blaine was the primary drummer behind the group of studio musicians called the Wrecking Crew.[1]**

You also get a new citation in the References section that looks like this:

**Miller, Michael (2005).** *The Complete Idiot's Guide to Playing Drums, 2nd Edition.* **Alpha Books. ISBN 1592574378.**

> NOTE: **Citations**
> Learn more about creating citations in the "Citing Sources" section later in this lesson.

For citations to work, you need to create a References or Notes section at the bottom of your article. You do so by using the following code:

```
== References ==
<references/>
```

This automatically inserts all your references into the section; no manually entry is required on your part.

# Text Formatting

Wikipedia offers many different ways to format the text within an article. Most of these formatting effects are generated by surrounding the affected text with some sort of code. For example, to format text as italic, you enter two apostrophes (*not* a single quotation mark) before and after the text; to format text as bold, you enter three apostrophes before and after the text.

The most common options are described in Table 9.1

**TABLE 9.1**   Wiki Markup Language Text Formatting

| Formatting | Markup |
| --- | --- |
| Italics | ''text'' |
| Bold | '''text''' |
| Italics and bold | '''''text''''' |
| Underline | <u>text</u> |
| Small text | <small>text</small> |
| Big text | <big>text</big> |
| Strikeout | <s>text</s> |
| Subscript | <sub>text</sub> |
| Superscript | <sup>text</sup> |

# Variables

Some information you place within an article is variable. For example, you might want to insert today's date or the name of the article. Rather than typing all the information (and running the risk of getting it wrong), Wikipedia lets you insert codes for variables like these. Just insert the code (typically a word within double brackets), and Wikipedia automatically generates the correct information.

Table 9.2 details some of the more common variable codes.

**TABLE 9.2**   Wiki Markup Language Variables

| Variable | Markup |
|---|---|
| Current year | {{CURRENTYEAR}} |
| Current month (number) | {{CURRENTMONTH}} |
| Current month (name) | {{CURRENTMONTHNAME}} |
| Current week | {{CURRENTWEEK}} |
| Current day (number) | {{CURRENTDAY}} |
| Current day of week (name) | {{CURRENTDAYNAME}} |
| Current time (hours:minutes) | {{CURRENTTIME}} |
| Current page name | {{PAGENAME}} |
| Current URL | {{fullurl:pagename}} |
| Name of site (Wikipedia) | {{SITENAME}} |

# Categorizing an Article

Most articles should be placed within a specific topic category on the Wikipedia site. To do so, enter the following code anywhere in the body of the article. This code categorizes the article and does not display within the article text.

```
[[Category:Category name]]
```

# Comments

To enter nondisplaying comments anywhere within the article's underlying markup, enter this code:

```
<!-- comment -->
```

# Table of Contents

One thing you don't have to worry about is coding a table of contents (TOC) for an article. Wikipedia automatically generates a TOC and places it on the page when there are at least four headings within an article.

> TIP: **Tables**
>
> Some information is best presented in tabular fashion. To insert a table into a Wikipedia article, use established HTML table tags (**<table>**, **<tr>**, **<td>**, and so on). Learn more at en.wikipedia.org/wiki/Help:Table.

# Citing Sources

All essential information within a Wikipedia article needs to be fully sourced. This means adding a citation to the article that points to the source.

> NOTE: **Sources**
>
> Learn more about citations in Lesson 5, "Verifying Information and Checking Resources."

As you previously learned in this lesson, you create a citation using the **<ref>** code. But what information should the citation contain?

It all depends on what type of source you cite. Table 9.3 presents three common types of sources and appropriate citation content and format.

**TABLE 9.3**    Citation Formats

| Source | Citation |
| --- | --- |
| Book | Author last name, author first name. *Title of book.* (Date of publication) Publisher. ISBN. |
| Newspaper or magazine article | Author last name, author first name. "Title of Article." *Name of newspaper.* Date of publication, page numbers. |
| Journal | Author last name, author first name. (Date of publication). "Title of Article." *Journal name.* Issue number, page number. |
| World Wide Web articles | Author last name, author first name. "Title of Article." Name of website. Date of publication or date article was retrieved. |

So, for example, if you cite my book *Selling Online 2.0*, you use the following citation:

**Miller, Michael. *Selling Online 2.0*. (2009) Que. ISBN 0789739747.**

# Summary

In this lesson, you learned how to edit existing Wikipedia articles. In the next lesson, you learn to create new articles.

# LESSON 10

# Contributing a New Article

*In this lesson, you learn how to create a new Wikipedia article.*

## Is the Topic Available?

With close to 3 million articles in the Wikipedia, it would seem as if just about every topic is covered. But that's not the case; chances are, you can find some topic of interest to you that does not have an article yet.

In this instance, you might want to contribute a new article to Wikipedia on that topic. To create an article, you must first register with and log onto the Wikipedia site. Then you can choose a topic you like and write the article.

Before you write an article, however, you need to make sure that there is no existing article on that topic. You do this by searching Wikipedia for that topic. If an article appears, there's no need to create a new one. But if no matching article appears in the search results, you're free to write a new article.

---

TIP: **Notability**

Wikipedia articles should be on "notable" topics. That is, the topic should be worthy of notice—meaning that it has received significant coverage in reliable sources that are independent of the subject.

---

# Creating the Article

How do you create an article for Wikipedia? As noted previously, it all starts with a search. Just follow these steps:

1. Search Wikipedia for the topic you want to write about.

2. If no article matches your search, Wikipedia displays the page shown in Figure 10.1. Click the red link for the article's title in the "You may create the page" text.

3. Wikipedia now displays the new article page, as shown in Figure 10.2. Enter the text of your article into the editing box.

4. When you finish writing the article, enter a summary of your article into the Edit Summary box.

5. Click the Save Page button when done; this places your newly written article on the Wikipedia site.

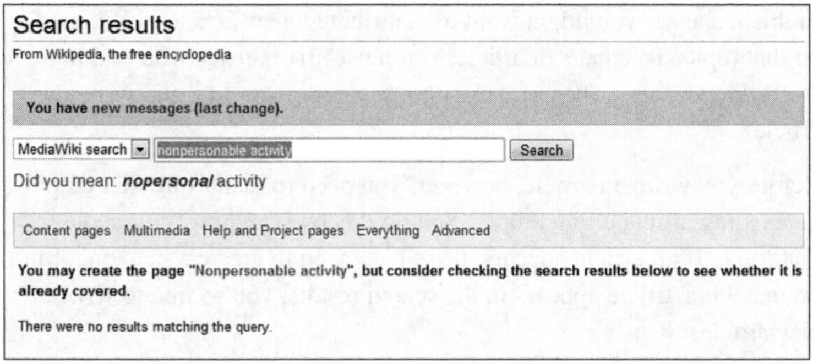

**Search results**

From Wikipedia, the free encyclopedia

**You have new messages (last change).**

| MediaWiki search ▾ | nonpersonable activity | Search |

Did you mean: *nopersonal* activity

Content pages   Multimedia   Help and Project pages   Everything   Advanced

**You may create the page "Nonpersonable activity", but consider checking the search results below to see whether it is already covered.**

There were no results matching the query.

**FIGURE 10.1**    What you see when no article matches your search.

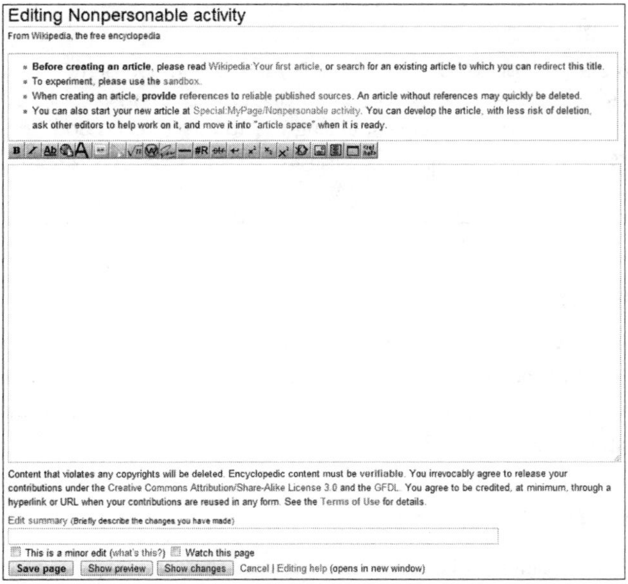

**FIGURE 10.2** Creating a new article.

When you write your article, use the toolbar at the top of the edit box to format your text and insert special elements. You can also insert codes from the Wiki Markup Language directly into your text; Wikipedia interprets these codes and inserts the appropriate formatting or elements.

> NOTE: **Wiki Markup Language**
> Learn more about the Wiki Markup Language in Lesson 9, "Editing an Existing Article."

# Structuring the Article

When constructing your article, it should follow standard Wikipedia article structure. We discuss each part of the article next.

> TIP: **Writing Style**
> When creating an article, make sure you write in complete sen-
> tences and in standard paragraphs. Use acceptable grammar and
> punctuation, and avoid personalizing the topic—that is, don't use
> the word "I." Write as if you're creating a term paper for a class or a
> research paper for your company.

## Summary

The summary is one or more paragraphs at the beginning that describe the
full content of the article. You don't need to do anything special to format
the summary; any text that appears before your first section head displays
as the summary.

## Table of Contents

The table of contents (TOC) appears between the summary and the main
body of the article. Wikipedia generates the TOC automatically as you
create sections within your article; you don't need to enter anything.

## Sections and Section Headings

Longer articles should be divided into shorter sections, each with its own
heading. Think of sections the same way you'd outline the article; each
part of the outline is a separate section in the article.

Naturally, each section has its own heading. You format the section heading by putting two equal signs (==) around the heading text, like this:

```
== Section Heading ==
```

You can also create subsections within major sections, with their own subheadings. To create a subheading under a major section heading, surround
the heading with *three* equal signs (===), like this:

```
=== Sub-Section Heading ===
```

## Images

If your article needs to be visually illustrated, then upload and insert appropriate images into the article. You can insert photographs, drawings, graphs, maps, and the like—anything you have the rights for (or is in the public domain), you can upload.

> NOTE: **Images**
>
> Learn more about uploading and inserting images in Lesson 11, "Incorporating Pictures and Other Media in Your Article."

## Citations

You need to cite sources for key information within your article. Enter these citations immediately after the appropriate text, using the **<ref>** code, like this:

```
<ref>citation details</ref>
```

> NOTE: **Citations**
>
> Learn more about creating citations in Lesson 9, "Editing an Existing Article."

To make your references appear in a References or Notes section at the end of the article, you have to first create that section. You do so by inserting the following code near the bottom of the page markup:

```
== References ==
<references/>
```

Your references now automatically appears as footnotes in the text, with the full citations in the Notes or References section at the bottom of the article.

## Appendixes

Your article can also include, at the end, one or more of the standard appendixes:

▶ **References**—Notes relating to the main text

▶ **Bibliography**—A list of related books

▶ **See Also**—A list of related Wikipedia articles

▶ **External Links**—Links to other pages on the Web

# Tips for Writing a New Article

Writing an authoritative article takes knowledge of the topic and mastery of the Wiki Markup Language. Here are some tips to keep in mind:

▶ **Do your research before you start writing**—You don't want to waste time looking up information while you have the editing page open.

▶ **Gather your references**—You must reference sources for all important information you include in your article. Make sure you have your references handy so that you can enter them as citations in your article.

> CAUTION: **Reliable Sources**
> Articles that do not adequately cite reliable sources are likely to be deleted.

▶ **Get organized**—Organize your article in standard Wikipedia fashion. That means creating a summary up front, dividing longer articles into separate sections (with separate headings), and including See Also and External Links sections at the end. You should also place your article in at least one relevant category.

▶ **Use the sandbox**—Want to see the result of various Wiki Markup Language codes? Then use the sandbox, a sort of Wikipedia practice page located at en.wikipedia.org/wiki/Wikipedia:Sandbox. The sandbox looks like a regular Wikipedia article, but because it gets "cleaned" every 12 hours, it lets you experiment with your code before you use it in a new article.

▶ **If you don't get it perfect the first time, edit it**—Because Wikipedia articles can always be edited, don't worry about getting your article perfect the first go round. You can always edit the article at a later time to correct mistakes or add more information.

▶ **Too short is too bad**—Don't write single-sentence articles or articles that contain nothing but a single Web link. Your article needs a little heft to be of value to other users.

▶ **Don't plagiarize**—It's not a good idea to copy information verbatim from other sources. This means you cannot just cut and paste info from a press release, book, or CD liner notes. Your article has to be original—even if you cite existing sources.

▶ **Don't write about yourself**—You should not contribute articles about your company, your band, or yourself. Your articles should not be self-serving, nor should they be advertisements or press releases.

▶ **Remember: It's an encyclopedia**—Write an article that wouldn't look out of place in a traditional encyclopedia. That means avoiding topics of narrow interest, instead writing about topics with depth and wide appeal.

# Summary

In this lesson, you learned how to write a new article. In the next lesson, you learn to insert pictures and other media into your article.

# LESSON 11

# Incorporating Pictures and Other Media in Your Article

*In this lesson, you learn how to upload and add media files to your Wikipedia articles.*

## Uploading Pictures and Other Media Files

You can enhance your articles by incorporating pictures, audio clips, and even videos into the text. Before you add a media file to an article, however, you first need to upload the file to Wikimedia Commons—Wikipedia's shared repository for media files of all types.

> NOTE: **Wikimedia Commons**
> Learn more about using Wikimedia Commons in Lesson 12, "Finding Pictures in the Wikimedia Commons."

To upload a media file, you first need to be logged on to Wikipedia as a registered user. You also need to be an *autoconfirmed* user, which happens automatically after you make at least 10 edits to other articles.

When you're an autoconfirmed user, follow these steps:

1. Go to the Special Upload page at en.wikipedia.org/wiki/Special:Upload, as shown in Figure 11.1.

2. Click the Choose File button.

3. When the Open dialog box appears, navigate to and select the file you want to upload; then click the Open button.

4. Enter the name of the file into the Destination Filename box.

5. Enter information about the image and the image file into the Summary box.

6. Pull down the Licensing list and select the type of license granted to the image file.

7. Click the Upload File button.

The file is now added to the Wikimedia Commons database and is available for inclusion in Wikipedia articles.

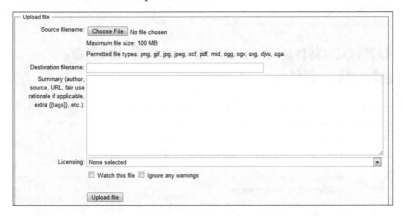

**FIGURE 11.1**    Uploading a file.

---

CAUTION: **Image Rights**

Wikipedia will accept only images that are in the public domain or that have a free license, such as that from Creative Commons. You cannot upload images that are copyrighted and for which you do not have explicit permission to upload.

---

NOTE: **Creative Commons**

Learn more about Creative Commons licensing at www.creativecommons.org.

# Image Formats

What image format should you use for the images you upload and insert in your articles? Here's the approved list:

- For photographic images, use JPG-format files.

- For drawings and line-art illustrations, use SVG-format files.

- For nonvector drawings and illustrations, use PNG-format files.

You should *avoid* using images in the BMP, GIF, and TIFF file formats. You should convert BMP and GIF files to the PNG format and TIFF files to the JPG format.

# Adding Images to Your Article

You use the Wiki Markup Language to add an image to an article. Enter the appropriate code in your article text in which you want the image to appear.

## Basic Images

There are several different ways for an image to display in your article. The most basic code inserts the image on the right side of the article page, as shown in Figure 11.2. Insert this code at the front of the paragraph that you want to appear beside the image:

```
[[Image:imagename.jpg|thumb]]
```

The blue tang is a perfect fish for the home saltwater aquarium. It's a peaceful fish, very seldom aggressive to its tank mates. While it is sometimes prone to ich on initial import, buying a seasoned speciman should mitigate the risk both to the tank and to your other fish. As with all tangs, you should not have more than one blue per tank, and should avoid more than one additional member of the tang species, as they can become aggressive towards other tangs. They eat mysis shrimp as well as all manner of greens; a varied diet is best. It's also advisable to include many hiding places in your tank, as the blue tang can be a tad shy, especially when first introduced and if there are more aggressive fish in the aquarium.

Other popular tangs include the yellow tang (smaller than the blue), the purple tang, and the sailfin tang (larger than the blue).

**FIGURE 11.2**   A basic image aligned to the right of the article.

Naturally, replace *imagename.jpg* with the actual filename of the image.

To add a caption beneath the image, like the one in Figure 11.3, use this code:

```
[[Image:imagename.jpg|thumb|caption text]]
```

Obviously, replace *caption text* with your own caption.

**FIGURE 11.3**    An image with a caption beneath.

> CAUTION: **Case Sensitive**
> Image names are case sensitive. For example, entering Picture.jpg
> will not retrieve a file named picture.jpg or PICTURE.jpg.

## Aligning the Image

By default, images are inserted on the right side of the article's text. You can, however, choose to position the image on the left side of the page, instead. Use this code:

```
[[Image:imagename.jpg|left]]
```

Also by default, the text wraps around the image. If you'd rather have the image appear on its own line, with text above and below, as shown in Figure 11.4, use this code:

```
[[Image:imagename.jpg|none]]
```

The blue tang is a perfect fish for the home saltwater aquarium. It's a peaceful fish, very seldom aggressive to its tank mates. While it is sometimes prone to ich on initial import, buying a seasoned speciman should mitigate the risk both to the tank and to your other fish. As with all tangs, you should not have more than one blue per tank, and should avoid more than one additional member of the tang species, as they can become aggressive towards other tangs. They eat mysis shrimp as well as all manner of greens; a varied diet is best. It's also advisable to include many hiding places in your tank, as the blue tang can be a tad shy, especially when first introduced and if there are more aggressive fish in the aquarium.

Other popular tangs include the yellow tang (smaller than the blue), the purple tang, and the sailfin tang (larger than the blue).

**FIGURE 11.4**   An image without text wrapping.

# Creating a Photo Gallery

If you have multiple images within a single article that are best displayed together (rather than spread throughout the body of the article), you can create a photo gallery of these images, like the one shown in Figure 11.5. Here's the code to use:

```
<gallery>
Image:filename1.jpg
Image:filename2.jpg
Image:filename3.jpg
Image:filename4.jpg
</gallery>
```

**FIGURE 11.5**   A multi-image photo gallery.

Note that when you insert filenames between the **<gallery>** and **</gallery>** codes, they are not surrounded with the normal double square brackets. You can add as many filenames as you want in the gallery.

# Inserting Audio Files

You can also insert audio files into your article. These files appear as shown in Figure 11.6 and play back when readers click the Play button.

**FIGURE 11.6**   An audio file embedded in an article.

Wikipedia accepts audio files in the Ogg Vorbis (.OGG) file format only. To listen to Ogg Vorbis files, users must have a compatible audio player installed on their computers.

> CAUTION: **MP3 Files**
>
> Wikipedia does not support the popular MP3, WMA, or AAC (iTunes) audio file formats.

To embed an audio file, you first have to upload it to Wikimedia Commons, as previously described in this lesson. You then insert the following code within the text of your article, where you want the audio player box to appear:

```
{{Listen¦filename=filename.ogg¦title=Title¦description=
Description}}
```

Obviously, replace *filename.ogg* with the actual filename, *Title* with the actual title, and *Description* with an actual description of the file.

> NOTE: **Templates**
>
> This code for embedding an audio file uses a Wikipedia *template*—a piece of code that automatically creates certain types of complex elements. For a list of popular templates, see en.wikipedia.org/wiki/Wikipedia:Template_messages.

# Inserting Video Files

Embedded videos, like the one in Figure 11.7, are much less common in Wikipedia articles than images and audio files. That's partly because Wikipedia accepts only video files in the relatively obscure Ogg Theora (.OGV) file format. So you must first convert your videos to the .OGV format before uploading.

B-47A, historical Video

**FIGURE 11.7**    A video player embedded in a Wikipedia article.

CAUTION: **OGV Files**

Not all video editing programs convert files to the OGV format, nor do all video player programs play back videos in this format.

When uploaded, you embed your video by inserting the following code where you want the video player window to appear:

```
[[File:filename.ogv|Caption text]]
```

Replace *filename.ogv* with the actual filename and *Caption text* with the text you want to appear under the video player.

# Summary

In this lesson, you learned how to insert pictures, sounds, and videos into the text of a Wikipedia article. In the next lesson, you learn to find photos and other media in the Wikimedia Commons.

# LESSON 12

# Finding Pictures in the Wikimedia Commons

*In this lesson, you learn how to upload and download media files in the Wikimedia Commons.*

## Understanding the Commons

The *Wikimedia Commons*, often called just the *Commons*, is a central repository of media files—images, audio, and video. It's a project of the Wikimedia Foundation, the parent organization of Wikipedia and include more than 4.5 million media files.

Files uploaded to the Commons are available for free downloading for personal use and for use in Wikipedia articles. For a file to be uploaded to the Commons, it must be in the public domain or licensed for free use.

You access the Wikimedia Commons at commons.wikimedia.org. The main page of the site, shown in Figure 12.1, looks a lot like the Wikipedia main page. This page includes links to the Commons in different languages; a Picture of the Day and Media of the Day (typically a sound file); links to Featured Pictures and Quality Images (as voted on by users); and links to content by topic, location, type, and so forth.

**FIGURE 12.1**    The main page of the Commons.

The Commons also features a navigation pane on the left side of every page. This pane is similar to the Wikipedia navigation pane, with panels for Search, Navigation, Participate, and Toolbox.

# Copyright and Licensing

Only files that are free from copyright restrictions are allowable in the Wikimedia Commons. This includes files in the public domain and those that are legally licensed for free use by others.

By default, the creator of a photograph, audio clip, or video owns the copyright to that work. The copyright gives the owner exclusive rights to the work, unless expressly licensed to others. For this reason, files that are copyrighted cannot be used in the Commons without the permission of the copyright owner. Copyrights typically last the life of the creator plus 50 to 70 years, depending on the type of work.

> NOTE: **Intellectual Property**
> Intellectual property laws differ from country to country, thus the length of copyright also differs.

Works that have never been copyrighted, or that have had their copyrights expire, are considered in the public domain. Public domain works can be used by anyone for any purpose, including commercial purposes; they can even be edited or otherwise changed by other users. Because of the nature of copyright laws, many public domain works are older photos, typically taken before the 1920s or so.

Some copyrighted works are licensed for sharing by others, typically at no cost. Some licenses allow for private use only, some for private and commercial use (on for-profit websites, in books, on television, and so forth). Some licenses require the work to be used as-is, without any editing, whereas other licenses let users change the work as they want. Most licenses require attribution to the copyright holder, although some licenses allow works to be used without attribution.

The most common sharing licenses are those from the Creative Commons organization. Creative Commons offers a variety of different sharing licenses, for private or commercial use, with and without attribution, and so forth. Files tagged with a Creative Commons license can be uploaded to the Wikimedia Commons.

> NOTE: **Creative Commons**
> Learn more about Creative Commons licenses at
> www.creativecommons.org.

# Finding Media in the Commons

Media files in the Commons are organized by topic. You can find topic pages—and the accompanying images and other media—by either browsing or searching.

> NOTE: **Articles**
> The Wikimedia Commons hosts fewer articles than Wikipedia because only those articles with images, sounds, or videos are listed.

# Browsing for Media

To browse media files by topic, follow these steps:

1. From the Commons main page, scroll to the Content section at the lower right, as shown in Figure 12.2.

2. Click the link for the topic you want.

3. If necessary, click an appropriate subtopic on the following page.

4. The resulting category page, like the one in Figure 12.3, displays all the media files for that topic. Click a thumbnail to display a page for that image, sound, or video.

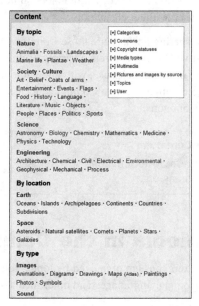

**FIGURE 12.2**    Browsing the Content section on the main page.

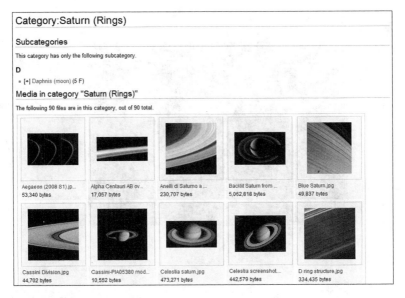

**FIGURE 12.3**    Media files on a category page.

# Searching for Media

You can also search for media files in the Wikimedia commons. To do so, follow these steps:

1. Enter your query into the search box in the navigation pane; then click Go.

2. You now see a page for the topic you queried, which includes thumbnails for all the media files for that topic. Click a thumbnail to display a page for that image, sound, or video.

# Viewing Media Files

Figure 12.4 shows a typical page for a media file, in this instance an image file. The page includes the following parts:

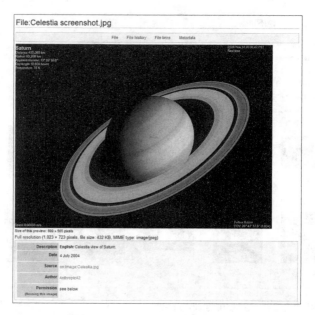

**FIGURE 12.4**   A typical media file page.

▶ The image itself, typically at a smaller size (to fit on the page);
  click the image to view it at full size.

▶ Information about the file, including a Description, the Date the
  file was created or the picture taken, the Source of the file, the
  creator (Author) of the file, and the licensing terms (Permission).

▶ A Licensing section, which details how the file can be used.

▶ The File History, which details when the file was uploaded and
  whether it was later edited.

▶ File Links—a list of pages (including Wikipedia articles) that
  link to this file.

▶ Metadata about the file (camera manufacturer, camera model,
  exposure time, and so forth) found with some digital photographs.

▶ Categories in which the file is associated.

# Downloading Files for Your Own Use

If you want to use a media file for your personal use in your website or blog, you can download it from the Wikimedia Commons. To download an image, follow these steps:

1. Go to the image page.

2. Click the image to enlarge it to full size.

3. Right-click the image and select Save Picture As (in Internet Explorer) or a similar option in a different Web browser.

4. When the Save As dialog box appears, select a location for the file and click Save.

When reusing media files outside the Wikipedia, know that you can use the files for any purpose, including commercial purposes if the source and authors are properly credited. You also need to license your version of the files—including any edits or improvements you make—with the same sharing license so that others can also use the files.

# Using Files in Wikipedia Articles

One popular use of Wikimedia Commons media is to include images, audio, and video in Wikipedia articles. You embed these files in an article using Wiki Markup Language codes.

For example, to include an image in an article, use the following code:

```
[[Image:filename.jpg|thumb]]
```

Replace *filename.jpg* with the name of the file, of course.

> NOTE: **Codes**
> Learn more about inserting image and other media files in Wikipedia articles in Lesson 11, "Incorporating Pictures and Other Media in Your Article."

# Uploading Files to the Commons

If you can download media files from the Commons, you can also upload files. To upload a file to the Commons, you must have rights to the file, and you must be a registered Wikipedia user.

> NOTE: **Reuse**
>
> Commons policy requires that any file you upload be licensed to be reused and modified for any purpose with or without your consent.

## Image Files

When uploading images, you need to follow some loose guidelines regarding image quality, file size, and file type.

In terms of image quality, the image should be as high a resolution as possible so that others using the image have the option to display at a high quality level. So if you have a choice between a low resolution and high resolution version of an image, upload the high resolution file. If you then use the image in a Wikipedia article, the MediaWiki software behind the Wikipedia automatically resizes the image as necessary.

> CAUTION: **PNG Resolution**
>
> The only restriction on image resolution comes with PNG-format images. Wikipedia's MediaWiki software cannot handle PNG images larger than 12.5 megapixels. It can handle JPG and other images larger than this, however.
>
> As to file sizes, you can upload image files up to 100MB in size—although there is a 6.5MB limit on image files embedded in Wikipedia articles. If you have a larger file you want to upload the Commons, you need to reduce the file size to meet Wikipedia's requirements.

As to file types, you should use JPEG-format files for photographs, PNG-format files for illustrations and computer screenshots, GIF-format files for animated images, and SVG-format files for line drawings, diagrams, and charts. You should *not* upload BMP- or TIFF-format images.

# Audio and Video Files

When uploading audio and video files, know that the Commons supports a limited number of file types. You can upload audio files only in the MIDI (.MID) and Ogg Vorbis (.OGG) formats, and video files only in the Ogg Theora (.OGV) formats. You cannot upload common file format such as .MP3, .MPG, and .WMV.

As to file size, the Commons accepts audio and video files up to 20MB in size. There is no restriction on audio bit rate or video resolution.

# Making the Upload

To upload a media file, you need to first logon to your account and go to the Commons main page. Then follow these steps:

1. Click the Upload File link in the Participate section of the navigation pane.

2. When the Commons: Upload page appears, as shown in Figure 12.5, click where the work is from—that is, what type of license applies to the work.

3. When the next page appears, read the legal information and then scroll down to the Upload Work section, shown in Figure 12.6.

4. Click the Choose File button to select a file from your computer's hard drive.

5. Enter the desired name for the file into the Destination Filename box.

6. Enter a description of the file into the Summary box. (More on this later in the "Describing Your File" section.)

7. Pull down the Licensing list and select the type of license that applies to the this file.

8. Enter one or more categories that should contain this file into the Categories box.

9. Click the Upload File button.

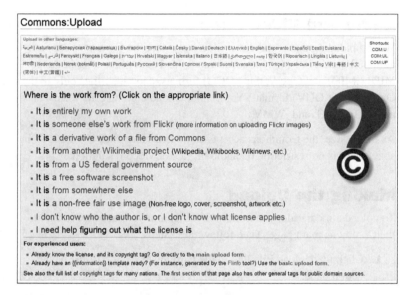

**FIGURE 12.5**    The Commons: Upload page.

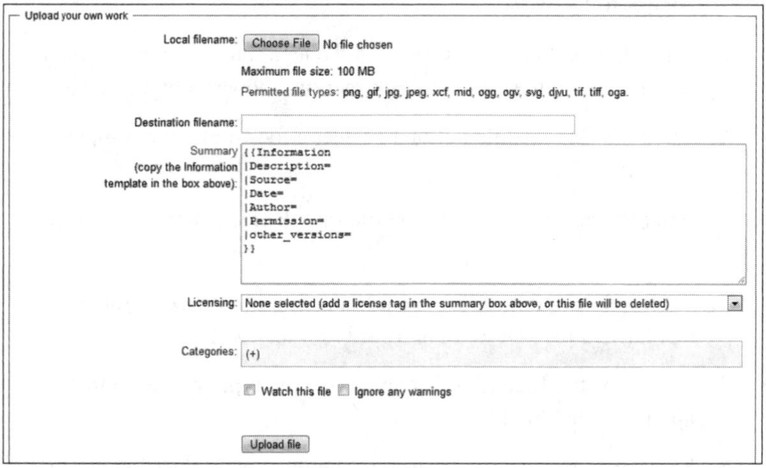

**FIGURE 12.6**    Entering information about a file.

# Describing Your File

The Summary section of the file upload form should include the following information:

- **Description**—A brief overview of what is in the file—what the image is of, what type of sound is involved, or the contents of the video.

- **Source**—Where the file came from.

- **Date**—The date the file was created.

- **Author**—Who created the file—that is, who shot the photo.

- **Permission**—The license associated with the file.

- **Other versions**—Any variations of this file also uploaded. For example, if you uploaded both low-resolution and high-resolution versions of a photograph, you would list the other filename here.

The easiest way to properly enter this information is to use the Information template available at the Commons site. Simply enter the following code into the Summary field; then enter your own information after each equals sign:

```
{{Information
|Description =
|Source =
|Date =
|Author =
|Permission =
|other_versions =
}}
```

# Summary

In this lesson, you learned how to use the Wikimedia Commons for uploading and downloading images and other media files. In the next lesson, you learn to ask questions of Wikipedia users via the Reference Desk.

# LESSON 13

# Asking Questions at the Reference Desk

*In this lesson, you learn how to ask and answer questions at Wikipedia's Reference Desk.*

## Understanding the Reference Desk

Have you been looking for information on Wikipedia but coming up short? Don't know where or how to look for specific information?

Then turn to the Reference Desk—a human-staffed part of the Wikipedia site that works like a reference desk at a traditional library. You ask your questions at the Reference Desk, and Wikipedia volunteers provide answers.

That's right, Wikipedia's Reference Desk works just like the one at your local library. The big differences between Wikipedia's Reference Desk and a traditional library reference desk are that Wikipedia's version is online (of course), and it's staffed by volunteers rather than paid professionals. In other words, your questions are answered by your fellow Wikipedia users.

To access the Reference Desk, as shown in Figure 13.1, scroll down Wikipedia's main page until you come to the Other Areas of Wikipedia section; then click the Reference Desk link. Alternatively, you can point your Web browser directly to en.wikipedia.org/wiki/Wikipedia:RD.

**FIGURE 13.1**    Wikipedia's Reference Desk.

What kinds of questions can you ask at the Reference Desk? Just about anything about anything. You can ask questions about specific topics covered in the Wikipedia, topics not yet covered, and about the Wikipedia itself. If another user—known as a *respondent*—knows the answer, you're in luck.

> CAUTION: **No Professional Advice**
>
> Wikipedia's Reference Desk is not a place to seek professional advice on medical or legal matters—although general medical and legal questions are allowed.

> CAUTION: **No Homework**
>
> Wikipedia's Reference Desk is also not a service to do homework assignments or write reports for others. Although you can ask questions about any topic, don't expect Reference Desk respondents to do the work for you.

What kind of answers can you expect from your questions? First, the good news: Researchers found that 92 percent of all questions were completely or partially answered—and quickly. The average time to a question's first response is 4 hours, with final responses coming no later than 72 hours after the asking.[1]

The bad news is that the answers you get are not always authoritative. The same research study found that the completeness of Reference Desk responses ranks just 63 percent, whereas accuracy level only ranks about 55 percent. Of course, you can improve the completeness and accuracy by asking follow-up questions; in most instances, improved answers result.

Remember, the people responding to Reference Desk questions are not necessarily experts in the topics at hand; they're just regular Wikipedia users, much like you. In this regard, the accuracy of Reference Desk answers is similar to that of Wikipedia articles. The information is only as accurate as the weakest respondent.

# Asking a Question

To ask a question at the Reference Desk, follow these steps:

1. Go to the Reference Desk home page, at en.wikipedia.org/wiki/Wikipedia:RD.

2. The Reference Desk home page is organized by category. Click the category into which your question falls.

3. On the next page, scroll down to the After Reading the Above section and click Ask a New Question by Clicking Here.

4. You now see an editing page for this section of the Reference Desk, like the one shown in Figure 13.2. Enter a subject for your question into the Subject/Headline box.

5. Enter the main text of your question, along with any necessary details, into the main editing box. Use the formatting toolbar or the Wiki Markup Language to format your text or add special elements.

6. Check the Watch This Page option.

7. Click the Save Page button.

---

[1] *Ayers, Phoebe, Dan Cosley, Pnina Shachaf, et al.* Understanding Information Work in Large Scale Social Content Creation Systems (October, 2007).

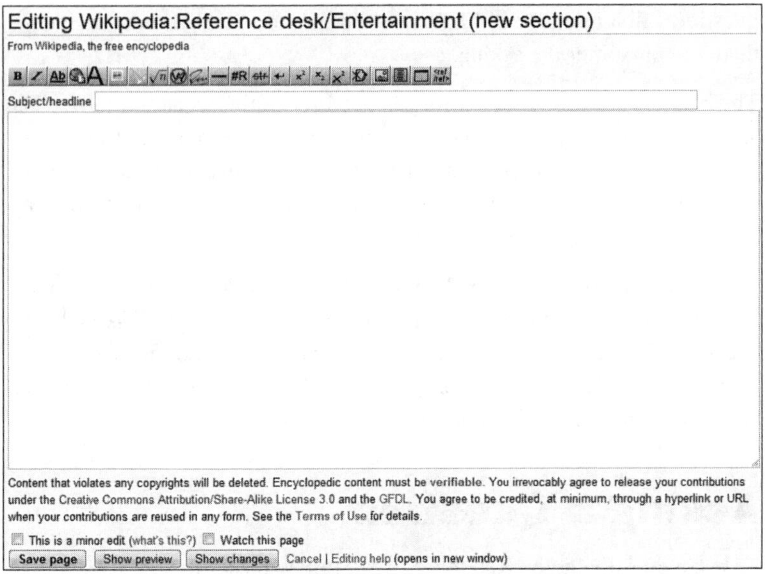

**Editing Wikipedia:Reference desk/Entertainment (new section)**

From Wikipedia, the free encyclopedia

Subject/headline

Content that violates any copyrights will be deleted. Encyclopedic content must be verifiable. You irrevocably agree to release your contributions under the Creative Commons Attribution/Share-Alike License 3.0 and the GFDL. You agree to be credited, at minimum, through a hyperlink or URL when your contributions are reused in any form. See the Terms of Use for details.

☐ This is a minor edit (what's this?)  ☐ Watch this page

[ Save page ]  [ Show preview ]  [ Show changes ]  Cancel | Editing help (opens in new window)

**FIGURE 13.2**    Entering a question at the Reference Desk.

Responses will be posted to this Reference Desk category page, under-neath the section that contains your question, as shown in Figure 13.3. If you checked the Watch This Page option when you entered your question, you'll be notified when changes are made to the page—that is, when responses are entered. Otherwise, you need to return to this page periodi-cally to check for new responses.

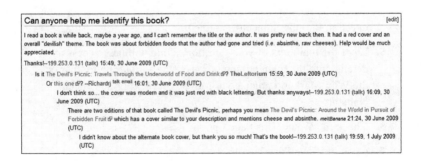

**FIGURE 13.3**    Responses to a Reference Desk question.

CAUTION: **Multiple Responses**
Any number of users can answer a single question—which might result in contradictory answers.

# Responding to a Question

Just as any Wikipedia user can ask questions at the Reference Desk, any user can also respond to questions asked by others. Whomever replies, Wikipedia expects answers that are factually correct, not opinions or guesswork. Ideally, answers should refer to relevant Wikipedia articles—or cite other reliable sources of information.

Most Reference Desk respondents tend to hang around a specific topic category, one in which they have some knowledge and interest. When they find a question that piques their interest, or that they actually know the answer, they respond. There is, of course, no obligation for respondents to respond to every question asked in a category.

To respond to a question, follow these steps:

1. From a Reference Desk category page, go to the section that contains the question you want to answer and click the Edit link.

2. When the Edit page appears, scroll to the bottom of the text in the edit box.

3. Enter your response into the Edit box, using appropriate Wiki Markup Language formatting. Make sure you indent your response and reference the source of the information you include.

4. At the end of your comment, enter four tildes (~~~~). Wikipedia replaces the four tildes with your user name and a time stamp.

5. Enter a summary of your changes into the Edit Summary box.

6. Click the Save Page button to save the revised article.

Your response now appears at the end of the section for the original question.

TIP: **Follow-Up Questions**

Many users ask follow-up questions after reading the initial responses. For this reason, you should return to the Reference Desk topic page on a regular basis to see if you need to provide further responses.

# Summary

In this lesson, you learned how to ask questions of other users via the Wikipedia Reference Desk. In the next lesson, you learn to look up definitions using the Wiktionary.

# LESSON 14

# Looking Up Words in the Wiktionary

*In this lesson, you learn how to use the Wiktionary to look up words and definitions.*

## Understanding the Wiktionary

The Wiktionary is a collaborative online dictionary and thesaurus. It's a sister project to the Wikipedia, from the parent Wikimedia Foundation. Like the Wikipedia, entries are provided and edited by the site's users. You use the site as you would any dictionary—to look up the spelling, definition, and usage of words.

The Wikimedia Foundation offers Wiktionaries in close to three hundred different languages. The English-language Wiktionary has more than 1.3 million entries, surpassed only by the French-language Wiktionary with more than 1.4 million entries. Other language editions are smaller.

You access the English-language Wiktionary at en.wiktionary.org. As you can see in Figure 14.1, the main page includes links to browse the Wiktionary by letter; a Word of the Day box; links to specific parts of the site; and a master search box.

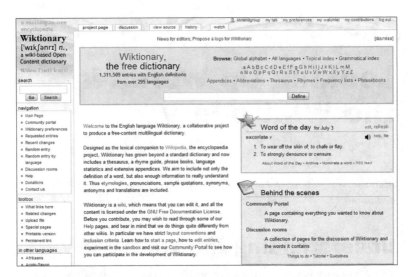

**FIGURE 14.1**    The English-language Wiktionary main page.

> **NOTE: Main Portal**
> The all-language Wiktionary portal is located at www.wiktionary.org.

The individual parts of the Wiktionary site include the following:

- ▶ **Main dictionary**—With entries contributed and edited by individual users

- ▶ **Abbreviations**—A list of common abbreviations and acronyms

- ▶ **Appendixes**—Short articles on a variety of related topics, containing relevant reference information

- ▶ **Frequency Lists**—Compilation of various "most common" and "most popular" lists

- ▶ **Phrasebooks**—Useful phrases in a variety of languages and dialects

- ▶ **Rhymes**—A short rhyming dictionary; displays words that rhyme with other words

- ▶ **Thesaurus**—A list of similar words

# Browsing the Wiktionary

You can look up words in the Wiktionary in two ways. You can browse the Wiktionary alphabetically, or you can search for specific words.

To browse the Wiktionary, follow these steps:

1. From the Wiktionary main page, click a letter in the Browse section at the top of the page (or in the Index section further down the page).

2. The next page lists entries beginning with that letter, like the one shown in Figure 14.2. Given the huge number of entries, each page contains only a fraction of available words; click the Next Page link to view the next words, alphabetically.

3. Continue clicking the Next Page link on subsequent pages until you find the page that contains the word you want.

4. Click an entry to view the page for that word.

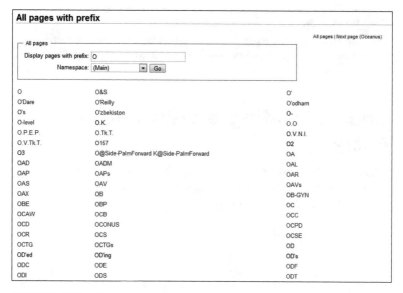

**FIGURE 14.2**   Browsing for words, alphabetically.

# Searching the Wiktionary

It might be easier to search for a word that you want. Just follow these steps:

1. From the Wiktionary main page, enter the word you're searching for into the search box at the top of the page, as shown in Figure 14.3.

2. Click the Define button.

The page for the word you searched for should now appear.

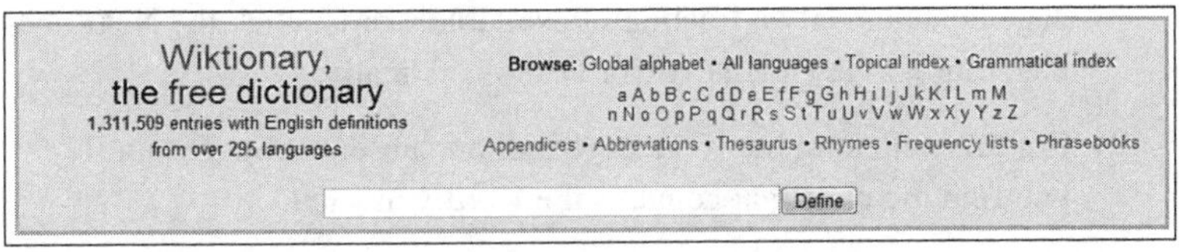

**FIGURE 14.3**   Searching for words in the Wiktionary.

> TIP: **Wildcards**
>
> As with the main Wikipedia, you can use wildcards (the * character) to better search for words of which you're unsure of the spelling.

# Understanding a Wiktionary Entry

Whether you browse or search for a word, Wiktionary eventually displays a page for that word, like the one shown in Figure 14.4. A definition page can include any of the following sections:

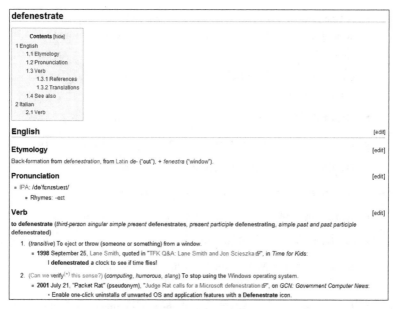

**FIGURE 14.4**   A Wiktionary definition page.

▶ **Entry name**—The word or phrase defined on the page.

▶ **Language**—The language of the word in question.

▶ **Pronunciation**—How to say the word.

▶ **Etymology**—The derivation of the word.

▶ **Homophones**—Words that sound like the word.

▶ **Rhymes**—Words that rhyme with this word.

▶ **Interjection**—When a word has no grammatical connection with the surrounding sentence and is used primarily to convey emotion.

▶ **Part of speech**—Whether it's a noun, a verb, or whatever. (Remember, some words can be multiple parts of speech.)

▶ **Inflections**—Any change in form for the word (usually by adding a suffix) that indicates a change in tense or grammatical function.

▶ **Definition(s)**—The meaning or meanings of the word. (A word can have more than one definition.)

▶ **Example sentences**—The word used in context.

▶ **Usage notes**—Advice on how to use the word in the real world.

▶ **Quotations**—Use of the word in famous quotations.

▶ **Synonyms**—Words that have a similar meaning.

▶ **Antonyms**—Words that mean the opposite of this word.

▶ **Derived terms**—Words or phrases derived from this word.

▶ **Related terms**—Words that have strong connections to this word—but that aren't directly derived from the word.

▶ **Coordinate terms**—Words that share a subordinate term with this word.

▶ **Descendants**—Terms in other languages that have borrowed or inherited the word.

▶ **Translations**—How the word or phrase translates into other languages.

▶ **Anagrams**—Words that share the same letters as this word.

▶ **See Also**—Other words that might be of interest.

▶ **References**—Sources of information about the word.

▶ **External links**—Other web pages with information about this word.

▶ **Category**—Which overall category this word belongs to.

# Contributing to the Wiktionary

You can create new Wiktionary definition pages and edit existing ones the same way you edit articles in the Wikipedia. In fact, you use the same Wiki Markup Language to format and insert elements into your entries.

## Creating New Entries

To create a new entry, follow these steps:

1. Enter the word you'd like to enter into the search box on the main Wiktionary page; then click the Define button.

2. If the word already exists in the Wiktionary, you see that word's page next. If the word doesn't exist in the Wiktionary, you see a page similar to that in Figure 14.5. Click the red link in the Create the Page text.

3. When the edit page for that word appears, as shown in Figure 14.6, enter the appropriate information for the word into the edit box. Remember to include all appropriate sections, using the == **Heading** == code for major headings and === **Subheading** === code for minor headings.

4. When you finish writing the entry, enter a summary into the Edit Summary box.

5. Click the Save Page button when done; this places your newly written article into the Wiktionary.

**FIGURE 14.5**   A page for a word without an entry.

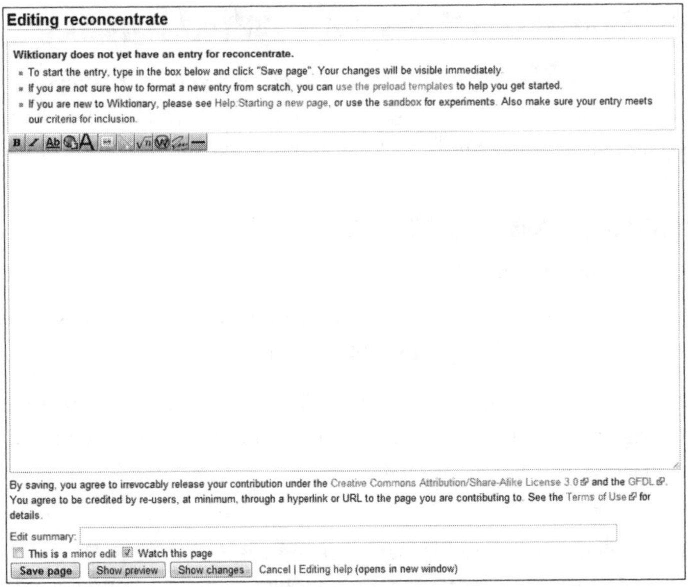

**FIGURE 14.6**   The edit page for a new word.

When you write the entry, use the toolbar at the top of the edit box to format your text and insert special elements. You can also insert codes from the Wiki Markup Language directly into your text; Wiktionary interprets these codes and inserts the appropriate formatting or elements.

> NOTE: **Wiki Markup Language**
>
> Learn more about the Wiki Markup Language in Lesson 9, "Editing an Existing Article."

# Editing Existing Entries

Editing a Wiktionary entry is similar to editing a Wikipedia article. When you see an entry that needs editing, follow these steps:

**1.** From the entry page, click the Edit tab.

2. This displays the edit page for the entry; make your edits to text within the edit box using appropriate Wiki Markup Language code.

3. Enter a summary of your changes into the Edit Summary box.

4. If this is a relatively minor edit (grammar, punctuation, formatting, and so forth), check the This Is a Minor Edit box.

5. Click the Show Preview button to preview the entry with your changes.

6. Click the Save Page button to save the revised entry.

# Summary

In this lesson, you learned how to look up words in—and add words to—the Wiktionary. In the next lesson, you learn to find famous quotations in Wikiquote.

# LESSON 15

# Finding Quotable Quotations with Wikiquote

*In this lesson, you learn how to use Wikiquote to look up famous quotations.*

## Getting to Know Wikiquote

Wikiquote is another fun project from the Wikimedia Foundation, a collaborative compendium of famous quotations. These include quotations from well-known people, books, films, and proverbs; some you're undoubtedly familiar with; others will be new to you.

Like other Wikimedia Foundations projects, Wikiquote is available in multiple languages—89 at last count. The English-language version of Wikiquote has more than 16,000 quotations listed. These quotations are organized both by topic and by source, so you can look up all of Mark Twain's quotations, for example, or quotations about politics.

You access the English-language Wikiquote site at en.wikiquote.org. As you can see in Figure 15.1, the main page includes links to browse the Wikiquote by type of quote, a Quote of the Day box, and links to selected and new pages on the site. There's also a navigation pane on the left side of all Wikiquote pages; this pane includes panels for navigation, category links, a search box, and site tools (Toolbox).

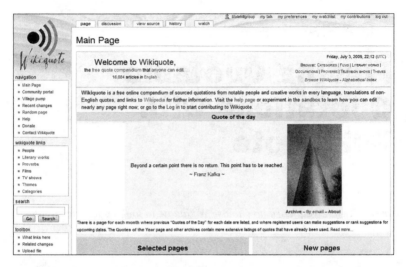

**FIGURE 15.1**    The English-language Wikiquote main page.

> NOTE: **Main Portal**
> The all-language Wikiquote portal is located at www.wikiquote.org.

# Looking Up Quotes

As with the main Wikipedia site, you can look up quotations in Wikiquote either by browsing or by searching.

## Browsing for Quotes

You can browse Wikiquote by topic or theme, by the person quoted, by type of production (films, TV shows, books, and so forth), or just alphabetically. You can even browse quotations that come from proverbs.

To browse Wikiquote by topic, theme or type of production, click the Browse Wikiquote link at the top-right part of the main page, as shown in Figure 15.2. When the Browse page appears, as shown in Figure 15.3, click the link for the category or person you want; continue clicking until you get to the desired quotation page.

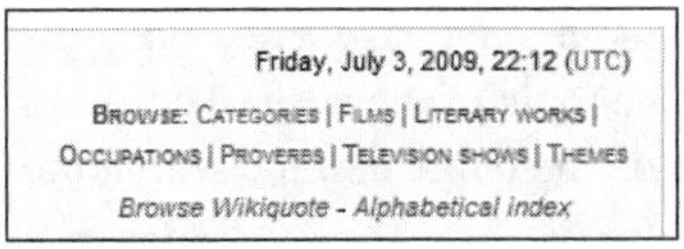

Friday, July 3, 2009, 22:12 (UTC)

BROWSE: CATEGORIES | FILMS | LITERARY WORKS |
OCCUPATIONS | PROVERBS | TELEVISION SHOWS | THEMES

*Browse Wikiquote - Alphabetical index*

**FIGURE 15.2**  Click Browse Wikiquote or Alphabetical Index to browse for quotations.

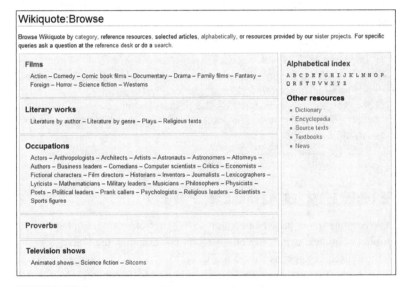

**FIGURE 15.3**  Browsing Wikiquote by topic or theme.

To browse Wikiquote alphabetically, click the Alphabetical Index link at the top-right part of the main page. When the Quick Index page appears, click the letter of the topic or person you're looking for; continue clicking until you get to the desired quotation page.

# Searching for Quotes

If you're looking for a specific quotation, searching might be the preferred method—especially if you know a few words from the quote. Follow these steps:

1. From the Wikiquote main page, enter one or more words from the quotation, the topic of the desired quote, or the name of the person who made the quote into the search box in the navigation pane.

2. Click the Go button.

The page that contains the quotation you're looking for should now appear.

> TIP: **Phrase Searching**
> If you search for a quotation that includes a specific phrase, enclose that phrase in quotation marks in your query. For example, if you search for a quote that contains the phrase "damned lies," (as in "lies, damned lies, and statistics"), enter the query **"damned lies"** in quotation marks.

# Viewing a Quote Page

A Wikiquote quote page can contain anywhere from a single quote to dozens of quotes, depending on the topic. For example, the Pierre-Auguste Renoir page, as shown in Figure 15.4, contains a single quote, whereas the John Adams page, shown in Figure 15.5, contains close to a hundred quotes from the founding father.

**FIGURE 15.4**    A page with a single quote.

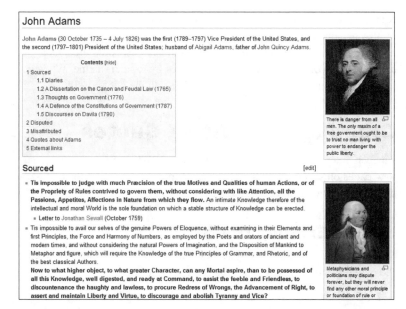

**FIGURE 15.5**   A page with dozens of quotes, organized by type of quote.

Some quote pages contain quotes about a particular topic. One good example of this is the Crime page, which offers Marcus Aurelius' famous quote, "Poverty is the mother of crime."

Other quote pages contain quotes from a particular work—a book, TV show, movie, or play. See, for example, the *As You Like It* page, with Shakespeare's famous quote, "All the world's a stage, and all the men and women merely players."

Then there are pages that contain quotes made by an individual, such as the aforementioned John Adams page and the Mark Twain page. From the latter are dozens of quotations by the famed humorist, including, "If you don't read the newspaper, you are uninformed; if you do read the newspaper, you are misinformed."

Quote pages are often divided into sourced, unsourced, disputed, and misattributed quotes. Sourced quotes are those that come from a specific source, such as a book or a speech. Unsourced quotes are those that have entered the public consciousness but don't have a definite recorded source. Disputed quotes are those that might or might not have been said by this person. Misattributed quotes are those that are thought to come from a person or work but really don't. Within each section, the quotes are sometimes organized by work, sometimes by topic or theme. When a quote has a source, it appears on the line beneath the quote itself.

# Creating and Editing Quotes

You can enter new quotations into any existing Wikiquote page, or create new pages on specific topics or works. The process is similar to creating and editing articles in the Wikipedia.

## Editing Existing Quotes

Wikiquote makes it easy to add new quotations to existing pages or to edit the quotations that appear there. Just follow these steps:

1. Go to the page you want to edit and click the Edit tab.

2. This displays the edit page for the entry, as shown in Figure 15.6. Make your edits to text within the edit box using appropriate Wiki Markup Language code. Make sure you insert any new quotes into the appropriate section of the page.

3. Enter a summary of your changes into the Edit Summary box.

4. If this is a relatively minor edit (grammar, punctuation, formatting, and so forth), check the This Is a Minor Edit box.

5. Click the Show Preview button to preview the entry with your changes.

6. Click the Save Page button to save the revised entry.

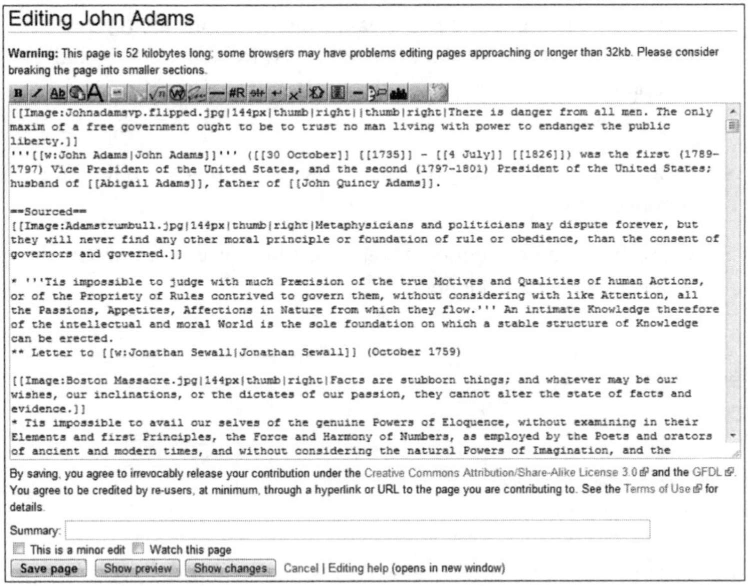

**FIGURE 15.6**   Editing an existing quote page.

> NOTE: **Wiki Markup Language**
> Learn more about the Wiki Markup Language in Lesson 9, "Editing an Existing Article."

## Creating New Entries

To create a new quote page, follow these steps:

1. Enter the topic or person you're writing about into the search box on the main Wiktionary page; then click the Go button.

2. If the topic already exists, you now see that topic's quote page. If the topic doesn't exist in Wikiquote, you see a page similar to that in Figure 15.7. Click the red link in the Create This Page text.

3. When the edit page for that topic appears, enter the appropriate information for the word into the edit box. Remember to include all appropriate sections, using the **== Heading ==** code for major headings.

4. When you finish writing the entry, enter a summary into the Edit Summary box.

5. Click the Save Page button when done; this places your newly written page into Wikiquote.

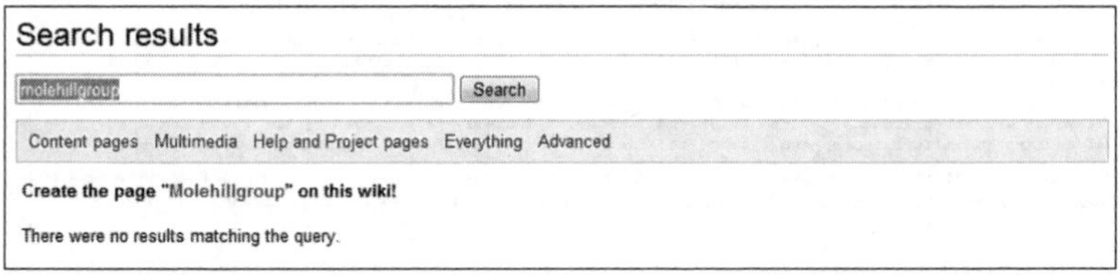

| Search results |
|---|
| molehillgroup    Search |
| Content pages   Multimedia   Help and Project pages   Everything   Advanced |
| **Create the page "Molehillgroup" on this wiki!** |
| There were no results matching the query. |

**FIGURE 15.7**   No page exists—you can create a new quote page.

When you write the entry, use the toolbar at the top of the edit box to format your text and insert special elements. You can also insert codes from the Wiki Markup Language directly into your text; Wikiquote interprets these codes and insert the appropriate formatting or elements.

# Summary

In this lesson, you learned how to use Wikiquote to look up quotations. In the next lesson, you learn to browse news articles with Wikinews.

# LESSON 16

# Getting the Latest News with Wikinews

*In this lesson, you learn how to read and write news articles on Wikinews.*

## Understanding Wikinews

Wikinews is a Wikimedia Foundation site that functions as a collaborative news aggregator. The site offers up-to-the-minute news articles, written by the site's users. Most articles aggregate facts reported by other sources; these sources are typically listed at the bottom of the Wikinews article.

Like the sister Wikipedia site, anyone can contribute or edit Wikinews articles. Unlike Wikipedia, Wikinews articles cover breaking news stories, with all information properly cited to ensure a high standard or reliability.

There are two types of articles on the Wikinews site. The most common type is called a *synthesis article* because it draws on reports from various media to synthesize the story covered. The other type of article involves *original reporting*; these are first-hand news reports written by Wikinews contributors. Of these two types, the synthesis article is the most common.

> NOTE: **Just the Facts**
> Wikinews articles contain factual reporting, not editorial opinions.

# Reading Wikinews Articles

The English-language Wikipedia home page, shown in Figure 16.1, is located at en.wikinews.org. This is like the front page of a newspaper, with the latest stories and headlines.

**FIGURE 16.1**    Main articles on the Wikinews home page.

At the top of the main page are links to Wikinews' main topics or sections: Crime and Law, Economy and Business, Politics and Conflicts, Science and Technology, Wackynews, and Weather. Beneath that are summaries of the days' top four stories; click the Full Story link to read each story in full.

Next up are several lists. On the bottom-left part of the main page is a list of the Latest News, with the newest stories at the top. Beside that are lists of the Most Popular Articles, Recent Interviews, and Original Reporting. A Stock Markets section and News in Pictures section are beneath those sections, with News by Country links beneath all that.

Browsing Wikinews is probably the best way to read the latest news; find a link to a story that looks interesting and then click the link to read the full story. You can also use the search box in the left-side navigation pane to search for news about specific topics or people.

Wikinews articles, like the one in Figure 16.2, are typically short. This is a "just the facts, ma'am" type of approach, with Wikinews contributors synthesizing the important details about a story from various sources. These sources are cited at the bottom of the article, in the Sources section.

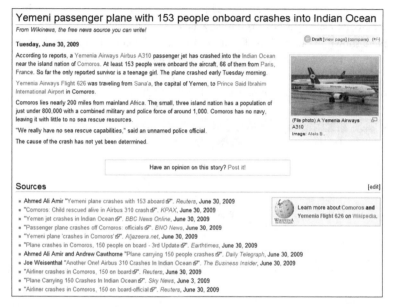

### Yemeni passenger plane with 153 people onboard crashes into Indian Ocean

*From Wikinews, the free news source you can write!*

**Tuesday, June 30, 2009**

○ Draft [view page] (compare)  (+/-)

According to reports, a Yemenia Airways Airbus A310 passenger jet has crashed into the Indian Ocean near the island nation of Comoros. At least 153 people were onboard the aircraft, 66 of them from Paris, France. So far the only reported survivor is a teenage girl. The plane crashed early Tuesday morning.

Yemenia Airways Flight 626 was traveling from Sana'a, the capital of Yemen, to Prince Said Ibrahim International Airport in Comoros.

Comoros lies nearly 200 miles from mainland Africa. The small, three island nation has a population of just under 800,000 with a combined military and police force of around 1,000. Comoros has no navy, leaving it with little to no sea rescue resources.

"We really have no sea rescue capabilities," said an unnamed police official.

The cause of the crash has not yet been determined.

(File photo) A Yemenia Airways A310
Image: Aleks B.

Have an opinion on this story? Post it!

**Sources**                                                                   [edit]

- Ahmed Ali Amir "Yemeni plane crashes with 153 aboard &". *Reuters*, June 30, 2009
- "Comoros: Child rescued alive in Airbus 310 crash &". *KPAX*, June 30, 2009
- "Yemen jet crashes in Indian Ocean &". *BBC News Online*, June 30, 2009
- "Passenger plane crashes off Comoros: officials &". *BNO News*, June 30, 2009
- "Yemeni plane 'crashes in Comoros' &". *Aljazeera.net*, June 30, 2009
- "Plane crashes in Comoros, 150 people on board - 3rd Update &". *Earthtimes*, June 30, 2009
- Ahmed Ali Amir and Andrew Cawthorne "Plane carrying 150 people crashes &". *Daily Telegraph*, June 30, 2009
- Joe Weisenthal "Another One! Airbus 310 Crashes In Indian Ocean &". *The Business Insider*, June 30, 2009
- "Airliner crashes in Comoros, 150 on board &". *Reuters*, June 30, 2009
- "Plane Carrying 150 Crashes In Indian Ocean &". *Sky News*, June 3, 2009
- "Airliner crashes in Comoros, 150 on board-official &". *Reuters*, June 30, 2009

Learn more about Comoros and Yemenia Flight 626 on Wikipedia.

**FIGURE 16.2**    Reading a Wikinews article.

> **NOTE: Main Portal**
> Wikinews is available in more than 20 different languages and countries. The all-language Wikinews portal is located at www.wikinews.org.

# Sharing a Wikinews Article

When you find a Wikinews article of particular interest, you can share it with friends and colleagues via social networking sites such as Facebook and Twitter. Underneath each article is a Share This box, like the one shown in Figure 16.3. Click the icon for the site you want to share on; then follow the directions for sharing the article on that site.

**FIGURE 16.3**    Click an icon to share a Wikinews article.

For example, to share an article via Facebook, click the Facebook icon in the Social Networks box. You're now taken to the Facebook site, with the page shown in Figure 16.4 displayed. Enter a brief comment about the article into the What's on Your Mind? Box and then click the Share button. Your comment, along with a synopsis of the article and link to the article on the Wikinews site, are now posted to the Wall on your profile page.

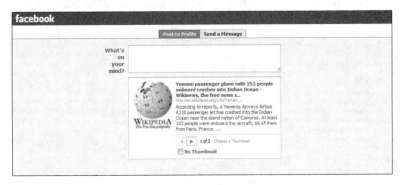

**FIGURE 16.4**    Sharing a Wikinews article on Facebook

To share an article via Twitter, click the Twitter icon in the Social Networks box. You're now taken to the main page of the Twitter site, as shown in Figure 16.5. A link to the Wikinews article is automatically entered into the What Are You Doing? box; click the Update button to post this link as a tweet.

**FIGURE 16.5**    Sharing a Wikinews article on Twitter.

# Writing and Editing Wikinews Articles

If you're a budding reporter, you can write your own Wikinews articles—or edit articles written by others. It all takes place in the Wikinews Newsroom, the hub of the site's news gathering operations.

## Writing a New Article

You enter the Newsroom by clicking the Newsroom link in the Navigation section of the Wikninews navigation pane. As you can see in Figure 16.6, this page lists articles in development, articles in dispute, and proposed articles. There is also a list of collaboration requests from other reporters and links to the Wikinews community.

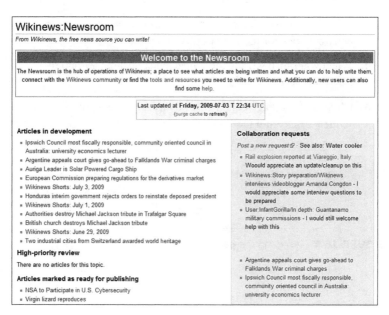

**FIGURE 16.6**   The Wikinews Newsroom.

---

TIP: **Check Before You Write**

Before you start a new article, search Wikinews to make sure the article doesn't already exist. You should also check the Newsroom to make sure the article isn't currently in development.

---

To write a new article, follow these steps:

**1.** From the Wikinews Newsroom, scroll to the Start a New Article section, shown in Figure 16.7, enter the name of the proposed article, and click the Create Page button.

**2.** When the article editing page appears, scroll down to the edit box (shown in Figure 16.8) and enter the text of your article. Use the formatting toolbar and Wiki Markup Language to format your article and include special elements.

**3.** At the end of the article, enter the **== Source ==** code and then enter citations for the sources of your article.

**4.** When you finish writing the article, enter a summary into the Edit Summary box.

**5.** Click the Save Page button when done; this places your newly written article onto the Wikinews site.

**Start a new article**

See Wikinews:Naming conventions/style guidelines for writing headlines; and the list of newly created articles first.

[                              ]

[ Create page ]

**FIGURE 16.7**    Entering the name of a new article.

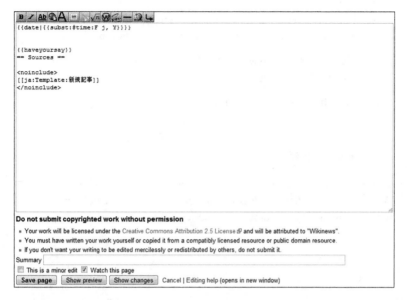

**FIGURE 16.8**    Writing a new Wikinews article.

NOTE: **Wiki Markup Language**

Learn more about the Wiki Markup Language in Lesson 9, "Editing an Existing Article."

# Editing an Existing Article

Because Wikinews operates in real time, not all articles posted are perfect. If you find an article that needs correction or elaboration, follow these steps:

1. From the article's page, click the Edit This Page tab.

2. This displays the edit page for the article; make your edits to text within the edit box using appropriate Wiki Markup Language code.

3. Enter a summary of your changes into the Edit Summary box.

4. If this is a relatively minor edit (grammar, punctuation, formatting, and so forth), check the This Is a Minor Edit box.

5. Click the Show Preview button to preview the article with your changes.

6. Click the Save Page button to save the revised article.

# Summary

In this lesson, you learned how to read, write, and edit articles on the Wikinews site. In the next lesson, you learn to read and edit books online with Wikibooks, Wikisource, and other collaborative sites.

# LESSON 17

# Reading and Editing Books Online

*In this lesson, you learn how to use the Wikibooks, Wikijunior, Wikisource, and Wikiversity sites.*

## Understanding Online Collaborative Books

As you've learned, Wikipedia is a giant online collaborative encyclopedia. But an encyclopedia is just one type of book; the Wikimedia Foundation offers several other sites that let you collaborate on different types of online books. These sites—Wikibooks, Wikijunior, Wikisource, and Wikiversity—operate in much the same fashion as Wikipedia, with the sites' users writing and editing the text that other users read.

An online book is like a Wikipedia article, only longer. As such, collaboration is essential; it's a lot easier for a hundred collaborators to create a 300-page book than it is for a single creator to do so. For this reason, the Wikimedia Foundation encourages collaboration on all these sites.

All the Foundation's online book sites work in similar fashion to the way Wikipedia works. You start a new book project by entering text into an edit box; you use the Wiki Markup Language to format the text and add special elements, such as headings, images, and links to other books and Wikipedia articles. After a book is started, other users can add more content or edit existing content by clicking the Edit This Page tab at the top of any book page.

A completed book—and some in-progress books—is often saved in PDF format. This enables readers to easily print a hardcopy of the book for reading anywhere. The PDF version also typically features more sophisticated formatting than the online version; many of these PDF books look and feel just like regular printed books.

# Using Wikibooks

The Wikimedia Foundation's main site for collaborative online books is Wikibooks (wikibooks.org). Wikibooks offers free textbooks and other texts edited by the site's user community.

Some books on the Wikibooks sites are original texts created by the site's users. Other books began as public domain or open source books, licensed for sharing, and were subsequently edited and expanded by Wikibooks users. All books on the Wikibooks site are covered by the GNU Free Documentation License, which enables free use by others.

> NOTE: **GNU**
> The GNU Free Documentation license is a form of copyright from the Free Software Foundation that provides the freedom for users to copy and redistribute a work, either commercially or noncommercially. Learn more at www.gnu.org/licenses/.

The focus of Wikibooks is educational—the creation of usable textbooks for students of all ages. Wikibooks are available on hundreds of topics in dozens of languages.

## Browsing and Reading Wikibooks

The Wikibooks home page, shown in Figure 17.1, contains links to browse books by category, the standard left-of-page navigation pane, and a list of featured books. From this page, you can find a book in several ways.

**FIGURE 17.1** The English-language Wikibooks home page.

One approach is to search by topic, using the search box in the navigation pane. Enter a query that describes what you're searching for; then click the Go or Search button. Clicking the Go button takes you directly to the best match for your query; clicking the Search button takes you to a full page of search results.

You can also browse for books from the main page. The Search and Browse box contains links to key topic categories; click a link to view all books in that category. Click a book to read it.

Another way to browse is to click the Browse link in the navigation pane. This displays the Card Catalog Office page, as shown in Figure 17.2. From here you can browse by subject, category, title (alphabetically), audience (reading level), and DDC (Dewey Decimal Classification) or LOC (Library of Congress) classification.

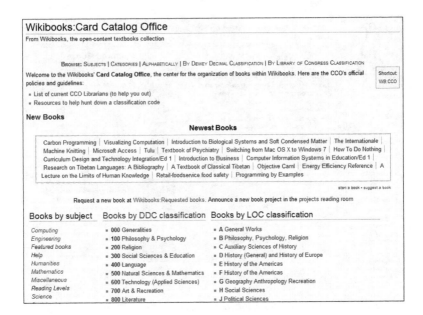

**FIGURE 17.2**   Browsing for books on the Card Catalog Office page.

When you open a book, it looks a little like a long Wikipedia article. The first page, like the one shown in Figure 17.3, typically contains the book's introduction or preface and table of contents. You access chapters in the book by clicking the links in the TOC. Each chapter displays on a subsequent Web page.

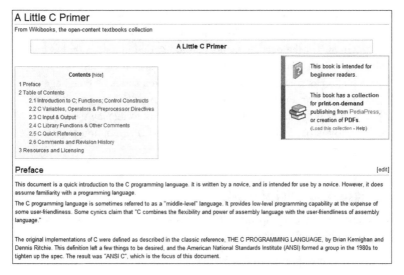

**FIGURE 17.3** The first page for a typical Wikibook—introduction and table of contents.

# Printing a Wikibook

All Wikibooks can be printed on your computer system's printer. How you print the book depends on the book's formatting:

▶ For those books that are in normal Web page format, simply click the Print button in your Web browser to print each page of the book individually.

▶ Some books are available in PDF format; you see a PDF link on the browse or search page that points to the book. Click the PDF link to display the book in formatted PDF format. You can then click the Print button in the Adobe Acrobat Reader software to print the entire book at once.

▶ Other books are available as so-called print-ready books. A print-ready book looks like a normal Web page but prints without any of the page elements that look good in a browser but are out of place on the printed page. Print-ready books are also formatted as a single Web page, rather than a series of Web pages, for easier printing. Look for a Printer-Friendly link when browsing or searching for a book; click this link to display the print-ready book, and then click your browser's Print button to print the book.

## Editing a Wikibook

Like articles in the Wikipedia, all Wikibooks can be edited by any user. To edit a book, follow these steps:

1. From the appropriate book page, click the Edit This Page tab.

2. This displays the edit page for that particular book or chapter, as shown in Figure 17.4; make your edits to text within the edit box, using appropriate Wiki Markup Language code.

3. Enter a summary of your changes into the Edit Summary box.

4. If this is a relatively minor edit (grammar, punctuation, formatting, and so forth), check the This Is a Minor Edit box.

5. Click the Show Preview button to preview the book chapter with your changes.

6. Click the Save Page button to save the revised book.

> NOTE: **Wiki Markup Language**
> Learn more about the Wiki Markup Language in Lesson 9, "Editing an Existing Article."

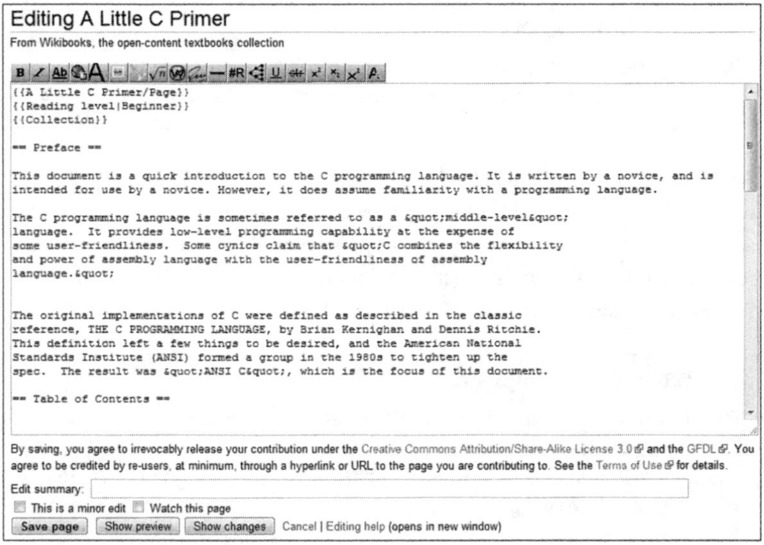

**FIGURE 17.4** Editing a Wikibook.

# Starting a New Book

Starting a new Wikibook is a bit more involved than creating a new Wikipedia article. First, you need to determine whether there's a need for that book, which you can do by visiting the Requested Books page (en.wikibooks.org/wiki/Wikibooks:Requested_books). Not every book idea makes for a good Wikibook.

Next, you have to plan the book, to think through its structure. This means creating a table of contents. Remember, readers need to quickly and easily browse through the book to find specific pieces of information; the TOC must take this browsability and findability into account.

Then comes the book title. Choosing a title isn't as easy as it sounds; the title needs to describe the book's content, without being vague or sensationalistic. Make sure the title reflects the common name for the topic and avoids unnecessary qualifiers ("for beginners," "introduction to," and so forth).

> CAUTION: **Title Don'ts**
>
> Your Wikibook title should *not* duplicate the name of an existing school course, nor should it include a subtitle or volume number.

After everything is planned out, you create a book similar to the way you create a Wikipedia article, using Wiki Markup Language to format the text and insert special elements. We won't go into all the detail here; you can read en.wikibooks.org/wiki/Using_Wikibooks/Starting_A_New_Wikibook for specific instructions.

> TIP: **Wikimedia Cookbook**
>
> One interesting Wikibook is the Wikimedia Cookbook, a massive collaborative online cookbook. You can access it by clicking the Cookbook link in the Wikibook navigation pane or by going directly to en.wikibooks.org/wiki/Cookbook.

# Using Wikijunior

Wikijunior is a subset of Wikibooks that offers free nonfiction books for kids from preschool up to age 12. These books are not only age-appropriate, but are also more visually interesting than traditional Wikibooks; the typical Wikijunior book contains lots of colorful photographs, illustrations, and the like.

You access the Wikijunior home page, as shown in Figure 17.5, by clicking the Wikijunior link in the Wikibooks navigation pane or by going directly to en.wikibooks.org/wiki/Wikijunior. From there you can browse the catalog by category or search for books on specific topics.

A Wikijunior book looks a lot like a series of Wikipedia articles. As you can see in Figure 17.6, there's a summary at the top of each chapter page, followed by a TOC for that chapter, followed by that chapter's text. There are typically lots of images to illustrate the topic and links to related topics.

## Welcome to Wikijunior

The aim of this project is to produce age-appropriate non-fiction books for children from birth to age 12. These books are richly illustrated with photographs, diagrams, sketches, and original drawings. Wikijunior books are produced by a worldwide community of writers, teachers, students, and young people all working together. The books present factual information that is verifiable. You are invited to join in and write, edit, and rewrite each module and book to improve its content. Our books are distributed free of charge under the terms of the Gnu Free Documentation License.

Please see What is Wikijunior and meta:Wikijunior for more information about this project.

At Wikijunior, we are writing books for children.

**Search Wikijunior:** (Template) (Discuss)

☑ Wikijunior   Search Wikijunior Now!

### Current Titles

There are currently more than a dozen Wikijunior books and hundreds of modules within those books being readied for publication. For information on creating new titles see the New Title Policy. You can also help decide which title should be developed next by voting.

### Just for KIDS

Wikijunior has some great books for you to read. But did you know that you can also help to write the books? If you know something about a subject and want to share it with other kids, just click on the link that says edit and type in what you want to say. It's that easy!

**FIGURE 17.5** The Wikijunior home page—Wikibooks for kids.

## Wikijunior:Dinosaurs/Tyrannosaurus

From Wikibooks, the open-content textbooks collection
< Wikijunior:Dinosaurs

*Tyrannosaurus rex*, or *T. rex* for short, was a dinosaur that lived on Earth about 65 to 70 million years ago, during the Cretaceous period. *T. rex* is one of the largest carnivorous (meat-eating) dinosaurs ever discovered.

*T. rex* from outside the Senckenberg Museum in Germany.

**Contents** [hide]
1 What was their body shape?
2 What did they eat?
3 When did they live?
4 What was their habitat?
5 How were they discovered?
6 What do we need to learn?

### What was their body shape? [edit]

*Tyrannosaurus rex* was up to 13 meters (42 feet) long, 5 meters (16 feet) tall, and weighed 4 to 6 tons (8,820 lb to 13,220 lbs.)- longer then a bus, and heavier then an elephant. It had a forward tilt, deep jaws, huge teeth, long tail, and tiny arms (also known as forelimbs). *T. rex*s jaw alone was about 1.3 meters long and had fifty to sixty bone-crunching teeth that were up to 10 centimeters long. Its arms were very stubby, no longer then a human being's. They were very strong, able to lift up to two hundred kilograms, but were not long enough to touch each other! *T. rex* stood on two powerful hind legs, each ending with a three toed foot, resembling a bird's foot, only much larger.

**Dinosaurs**

**Tyrannosaurus Rex**
Stegosaurus
Allosaurus
Apatosaurus
Pterosaurs
Triceratops
Plesiosaur
Ichthyosaur
Pachycephalosaurus
Velociraptor
Herrerasaurus
Ankylosaurus
Iguanodon
Brontosaurus

### What did they eat? [edit]

*T. rex* was a very big meat-eating dinosaur. It would have been at the top of the food chain. It is known to have fed on other large dinosaurs, such as Edmontosaurus, Anatotitan, and Triceratops, and probably could have swallowed smaller dinosaurs in a single bite.

One scientist believes that *T. rex* was a scavenger (an animal that eats already dead animals). He argues that it might not have been fast enough to catch prey. Other scientists believe that *T. rex* probably scavenged and

*T. rex* skeleton from the Smithsonian Museum of Natural History

**FIGURE 17.6** A typical Wikijunior book page.

Editing a Wikijunior book is similar to editing any Wikibook; just click the Edit This Page link and go from there. Similarly, you can create new Wikijunior books the same way you create new traditional Wikibooks.

# Using Wikisource

Where Wikibooks is all about collaborative book projects, Wikisource is a Wikimedia Commons site that offers existing books and other publications for free viewing or downloading. These are not collaborative works, but rather the original texts.

Wikisource offers books and other publications (including magazine and newspaper articles) that are available for unrestricted sharing. That means works in the public domain or those created with any free-sharing license. At present, there are more than 120,000 English-language texts in the Wikisource library.

> NOTE: **Wikibooks Versus Wikisource**
> Wikisource differs from Wikibooks in that Wikibooks are expected to be significantly modified by users; whereas Wikisource books typically contain only the original text of existing works.

As you can see in Figure 17.7, the English-language Wikisource home page (en.wikisource.org) includes links to indexes of works and authors, a list of new texts, a featured text, and the ubiquitous navigation pane. You can search the Wikisource library using the search box in the navigation pane, or browse works by topic or title. Works in the Wikisource library are typically fairly plain looking, just pages of plain text with few if any images.

Works are added to the Wikisource library by volunteers. Although users are encouraged to enter new texts into the library, they are not encouraged to edit any existing texts.

To add a new work to the library, you first need to check the text's copyright status; it needs to either be in the public domain or have a license compatible with the Creative Commons Attribution Share Alike 3.0 license. It's easiest to upload an existing text file than enter a complete manuscript by hand, so make sure the text is either in plain text or ASCII format.

**FIGURE 17.7**  The Wikisource home page.

---

NOTE: **Creative Commons**

Creative Commons is a nonprofit organization that promotes content sharing and collaboration. Learn more about the organization's various licenses at www.creativecommons.org.

---

CAUTION: **No Word Files**

Wikisource does not permit uploading of Microsoft Word-format documents because Word formatting codes are different from the codes used in the Wiki Markup Language.

---

Creating and formatting a new entry in the Wikisource library is similar to but slightly more complex than adding a new Wikipedia article. You can find more details of the process (including all the necessary formatting codes) at en.wikisource.org/wiki/Help:Adding_texts.

# Using Wikiversity

The Wikimedia Foundation offers one more source of collaborative online books. Wikiversity (www.wikiversity.org) is a project that creates online learning communities, complete with associated learning materials. Unlike Wikibooks and Wikisource, Wikiversity materials are tutorial in nature; it's actually a collection of online classes on various subjects.

As you can see in Figure 17.8, the Wikiversity home page, you can either search or browse for topics. You search for courses using the search box in the navigation pane. To browse for courses or course materials, use the links in the Explore Wikiversity box; you can browse by school level, subject, faculty members, or type of resource (activities, articles, lectures, lessons, and the like).

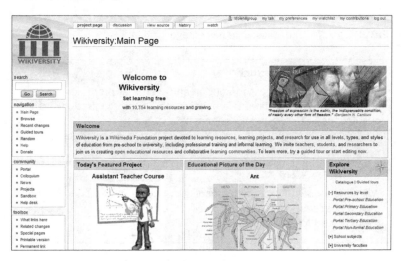

**FIGURE 17.8**    The Wikiversity home page.

Like other Wikimedia Commons sites, any user can create and edit Wikiversity courses and content; the process is similar to creating and editing Wikipedia articles. Learn more about contributing to Wikipedia (including teaching courses) at en.wikiversity.org/wiki/Wikiversity:FAQ.

# Summary

In this lesson, you learned how to read and edit online books at various Wikimedia Commons sites. In the next lesson, you learn to link to Wikipedia content on your own website.

# LESSON 18

# Linking to Wikipedia Content on Your Own Website

*In this lesson, you learn how to link to Wikipedia articles from another website or blog.*

## Why Link to Wikipedia?

Wikipedia is one of the most linked-to sites on the Web. That should come as no surprise because Wikipedia is the default authority on hundreds of thousands of topics.

Many websites and blogs link to specific Wikipedia articles. It's easy to do and can provide benefits to your site's readers.

Why would you want to link to a Wikipedia article? There are a number of reasons, including the following:

▶ Wikipedia provides additional information about a topic you're discussing.

▶ By linking to a Wikipedia article, you don't have to explain or provide extensive information about a particular topic; you let Wikipedia fill in the background for you.

▶ Because Wikipedia articles are constantly updated, you can be assured that your readers get the latest information about a topic—which you can't do unless you update your website on a daily basis.

▶ People are familiar with Wikipedia, so they're not afraid to click through and read the linked-to article.

In other words, you can use Wikipedia to provide information that you have neither the time nor knowledge to provide yourself. Just enter a link to a specific article within the text of your Web page or blog, and let readers click to read that article on the Wikipedia site.

# Creating a Link

Linking to a Wikipedia article is easy. Assuming that you're linking to the English-language version of Wikipedia, the URL for a Wikipedia article is constructed in this fashion:

```
http://en.wikipedia.org/wiki/articlename
```

If you know the name of the article, simply insert it in place of *article-name* in the URL. For example, if you want to link to the article about biology, use the URL **http://en.wikipedia.org/wiki/Biology**. If you want to link the article on North Korea, use the URL **http://en.wikipedia.org/wiki/North_Korea**.

Note that you must put the underscore character (_) between words in article titles that have multiple words. In addition, proper capitalization is important when linking to Wikipedia articles. You must capitalize the title in the URL exactly the same as the title of the article on the Wikipedia site.

To link to articles on other-language Wikipedia sites, replace the **en** in the URL with the prefix for that language's site. For example, to link to the Spanish language Wikipedia site, use the URL **http://es.wikipedia.org/wiki/*articlename***.

> TIP: **Copy and Paste**
> If you don't know the name of the article, you can use your Web browser to navigate to the article page and then copy the article's URL verbatim.

After you have the URL for the article, you insert the following HTML code into your Web page to create the linking text:

```
<a href="http://en.wikipedia.org/wiki/articlename">Link
text</a>
```

Naturally, replace *articlename* with the name of the article, and *Link text* with the text on your page that contains the link. For example, if you're writing about the FBI and want to link to the Wikipedia article named "Federal Bureau of Investigation," you might enter something like this:

```
The <a href=
"http://en.wikipedia.org/wiki/Federal_Bureau_of_Investigation">
FBI</a> is the agency that investigates domestic crime on a
national level.
```

CAUTION: **Revisions**

The link you create links to the current page for that article—not necessarily the page you read when you created the link. Even though Wikipedia articles are constantly updated, links to articles remain the same. So don't be surprised if you point to a version of an article that is slightly or significantly different from the original article you read.

# Summary

In this lesson, you learned how to link to Wikipedia articles. In the next lesson, you learn to use Wikipedia for academic research—or not, as the case might be.

# LESSON 19

# Using Wikipedia for Research and School Papers

*In this lesson, you learn whether and how to use Wikipedia when writing research papers.*

## Trusting Wikipedia—or Not

Given the breadth and depth of coverage offered, it's not surprising that many students, businesspeople, and even professional researchers use Wikipedia as a key research tool. But how reliable is the information you find in a typical Wikipedia article—and should you trust what you find on the site?

It's important to remember that Wikipedia is not written by a team of trained professionals. No single individual is responsible for maintaining the accuracy of the information within. There are no guarantees that what you read is a complete and accurate accounting of a given topic. It's a collaborative effort to which everyone is invited to contribute.

Knowing this, you might assume that the information presented in Wikipedia would be sketchy, unreliable, and even biased. Although that can—and does—happen, it's surprising to some that the average Wikipedia article is relatively complete, quite accurate, and free from partiality.

You see, the very thing that could cause unreliable results—the huge mass of nonprofessional contributors—actually works to increase Wikipedia's reliability. It's the sheer number of users that matters; the more eyes reading and vetting any given article, the more likely that any mistakes or inaccuracies will be discovered and then corrected.

That does not mean, however that every Wikipedia article is 100 percent accurate and fully comprehensive. Mistakes do creep into the article database, and some contributors are more informed and quality conscious than others. There are even, unfortunately, some contributors who deliberately enter false information, for whatever reasons.

And even if the Wikipedia community does a relatively good job at catching and correcting inaccuracies, at any given moment any given article might be in a precorrected state; that is, it's possible to catch a bad article before any factual errors have been found and fixed. There is no way to know whether an article has been fully fact-checked; you could be the first person reading an inaccurate article.

The bottom line, then, is that you can't assume that everything you read in Wikipedia is the ultimate truth. Although the vast majority of Wikipedia articles are accurate and comprehensive, some are not. And it's that one bad apple that can trip you up.

A cautious researcher, then, would not take any Wikipedia article as the final word on a topic. I like the approach of "trust but verify"—that is, use Wikipedia as a base for your research, but then independently verify the information you find there. It's all a matter of starting with Wikipedia but then going beyond that with your own verifiable research.

# Using Wikipedia as a Starting Point

It's interesting that even Wikipedia staff doesn't recommend using Wikipedia as the sole source of research. Sandra Ordonez, a former communications manager at Wikipedia, made the following recommendation:

**"Wikipedia is the ideal place to start your research and get a global picture of a topic; however, it is not an authoritative source. In fact, we recommend that students check the facts they find in Wikipedia against other sources. Additionally, it is generally good research practice to cite an original source when writing a paper, or completing an**

**exam. It's usually not advisable, particularly at the university level, to cite an encyclopedia."**

The point is not that Wikipedia is inherently unreliable; it's that Wikipedia is not a primary source of information. Wikipedia is, like any encyclopedia, a secondary source—it repeats (and cites) information revealed elsewhere. As such, Wikipedia is only as reliable as the sources it cites.

Think of it this way. Wikipedia retells stories that were reported elsewhere; Wikipedia doesn't do the reporting. It assembles information from a variety of sources but doesn't create any information of its own. It's a consolidator of information, not a creator—just like any traditional encyclopedia.

Wikipedia then should be thought of as a source of background information for the topic at hand, not the ultimate source of details. You can trust what you read in a Wikipedia article to a point, but you should always verify what you read.

# Researching Citations

This is why citations are so important in Wikipedia articles. By backtracking through the sources of information for an article, you can discover for yourself the primary sources—which often are more detailed and comprehensive than the extracts that find their way to Wikipedia. In addition, you can read the original sources to discover whether they support the information that was in the Wikipedia article; it's basic fact checking.

So the first thing to do when researching a topic via Wikipedia is to search out and read the sources cited in the article's Notes section. Many of these sources are available on the Web; others might need to be tracked down at your local library.

# Researching Additional Sources

Many Wikipedia articles include See Also, External Links, and References sections. These sections point to additional material relevant to the topic at hand, in the form of books, scholarly articles, websites, and the like. These references can be sources of either background or detailed information that might prove useful to your ongoing research.

TIP: **Further Information**

The sources listed at the bottom of a Wikipedia article can often lead you to additional books, periodicals, and websites about the topic. You should read all you can about a topic to conduct the most informed research possible; multiple independent sources increase the reliability of any information.

## Researching an Article's History

When it comes to background information, you can learn a lot by investigating the history of any given Wikipedia article. As information in an article gets added or changed over time, you cannot only get a feel for the overall quality of the content (and edits), but also for any controversy surrounding a topic.

NOTE: **History**

Learn more about article history in Lesson 7, "Tracking Changes to an Article."

Additional background comes from observing the discussions surrounding a given article. Most discussion pages reveal talks about what content should be included, debates about the accuracy and appropriateness of the content, even questions about sources, accuracy, and the like from other users. For that matter, you can use the discussion page to pose your own queries about the content in question. It's a useful background reference tool.

NOTE: **Discussions**

Learn more about Wikipedia discussions in Lesson 8, "Discussing an Article."

CAUTION: **Plagiarism**

You should never copy text from a Wikipedia article into any scholarly or research paper and try to pass it off as original work. Although it's okay to quote brief passages (properly cited, of course), reusing any existing text is plagiarism and will eventually be discovered.

# Referencing Wikipedia—or Not

As we discussed, Wikipedia can be a useful tool when you write a scholarly or research paper. But is Wikipedia a tool you should reference within the paper itself?

The answer is, probably not. In most situations, only primary sources are acceptable for citing within a research paper; secondary sources, such as Wikipedia, should not be cited.

## Wikipedia: Not a Primary Source

Wikipedia itself acknowledges that it shouldn't be cited as a source in academic papers. Here's what the site says:

**"In most academic institutions, Wikipedia, along with most encyclopedias, is unacceptable as a major source for a research paper."**

It's simply a matter of primary versus secondary sources. Primary sources—the original source of the information—can and should be cited; secondary sources—Wikipedia and other encyclopedias—should not. You want your paper to reflect as close a relationship to the primary sources as possible. Wikipedia is too far removed to be acceptable.

There are other reasons not to cite Wikipedia, of course. First, there's the issue of the changing nature of each article; when the text is in constant flux, the article you cite might have changed significantly since when you first read it. (Although you can call up and cite a specific version of an article using Wikipedia's history function, that still doesn't get around the fact that a more recent version of the article might be available—and might include different facts.)

In addition, there's the matter of credentials. The words of an anonymous, amateur contributor don't carry as much weight as the words of a respected academic or trained professional. Experience and title count.

Finally, know that many schools simply won't accept papers sourced partially or exclusively from Wikipedia. It's viewed as lazy scholarship, relying on a secondary source to essentially write the paper for you. If a teacher sees or senses that you based your paper on a Wikipedia article, you'll likely get low marks—or have your paper rejected completely.

> NOTE: **Secondary Sources**
>
> It isn't just Wikipedia; many teachers reject papers sourced from any type of secondary source, such as encyclopedias. As noted previously, primary sources are always preferred. It's the difference between saying "John Smith found" and "Bob Brown said John Smith found"; the first instance is primary information, whereas the second is the type of secondary information offered by Wikipedia.

## Citing Wikipedia

All that said, there might be instances where you are permitted or even encouraged to cite Wikipedia in your research. If you do cite a Wikipedia article, you need to cite a specific version of an article—that is, the article as it existed on a specific date.

In print, you do this by citing both the article name and the date the article was retrieved, like this:

```
"Article Title," Wikipedia (www.wikipedia.com), Article Date
```

So, for example, if you were citing the article on leptodactylidae (a type of frog) that you retrieved on July 3, 2009, you'd use this citation:

```
"Letodactylidae," Wikipedia (www.wikipedia.com), July 3, 2009,
```

For online papers, you can actually link to a specific version of an article by using that version's unique URL. To find the URL, click the Permanent Link link in the article's navigation bar; this reloads the page with a URL specific to the current date. In the case of our July 3, 2009, leptodactylidae article, the URL looks like this:

```
http://en.wikipedia.org/w/index.php?title=Leptodactylidae&oldid
=281771443
```

Clicking on this link always takes you to the April 4, 2009, version of the article.

## Summary

In this lesson, you learned how to use Wikipedia in research papers. In the next lesson, you learn to participate in the Wikipedia community.

# LESSON 20

# Participating in the Wikipedia Community

*In this lesson, you learn how to communicate with other Wikipedia users.*

## About the Wikipedia Community

The Wikipedia community is nothing more and nothing less than the users who either read or contribute articles to the Wikipedia site. Obviously, some community members participate more than others; it's fair to say that the bulk of the active community consists of those who create and edit Wikipedia articles.

As such, the Wikipedia community is diverse, encompassing everyone from professionals and academics to hobbyists to the merely curious. Users of all types can contribute to Wikipedia; there are no rules that prohibit anyone from doing anything.

That said, there is some perceived bias in the community, particularly in favor of frequent contributors. It's not surprising to find that most Wikipedia users are readers, not contributors; it's a lot easier to read an article than it is to write or edit one. It's a lot like the old 80/20 rule, but more extreme. As Wikipedia founder Jim Wales revealed (back in 2005), 50 percent of all Wikipedia edits were made by just 0.7 percent of users; 75 percent of all articles were written by less than 2 percent of the user base.

These numbers reveal that the active Wikipedia community is a lot smaller than you might think. It's understandable, then, for this active group to be somewhat self-centered, and not always accommodating to new or casual users.

That said, community plays an important role in maintaining the Wikipedia content. As with any wiki, communication and collaboration are key to encouraging the user input that is necessary to grow the knowledgebase of articles. Without active contributors, Wikipedia would eventually wither and die.

Working together, the Wikipedia community not only contributes new content, but also structures navigation between articles, resolves conflict between individual contributors, and creates the site's formal and informal rules of behavior. It's a self-policing community, but one that also, if only by necessity, continually welcomes new contributors to the fold.

# Welcome to the Community Portal

The home base for the Wikipedia community is the Community portal, as shown in Figure 20.1. You access this portal by clicking the Community Portal link in the Interaction section of the navigation pane or by going directly to en.wikipedia.org/wiki/Wikipedia:Community_portal.

**FIGURE 20.1**   The Wikipedia Community Portal

The Community Portal includes information and links of interest to the Wikipedia community, including the following:

- ▶ **The Community Bulletin Board**—Wikipedia-related news and announcements

- ▶ **Help Out**—A list of suggested activities for interested users, including a task list of articles that need work

- ▶ **Collaborations**—A list of open articles on which you can collaborate

- ▶ **The Wikipedia Signpost**—A community-written Wikipedia online newspaper

- ▶ **Wikipedia Weekly**—A once-a-week podcast highlighting Wikimedia Foundation staff

- ▶ **WikiVoices**—A user-created Wikipedia-related podcast

# Discussing Things at the Village Pump

When you want to discuss not individual articles but Wikipedia in general, the place to go is the Village Pump (en.wikipedia.org/wiki/Wikipedia:Village_pump). As you can see in Figure 20.2, the Village Pump is a communitywide discussion board—actually, a set of Wikipedia pages set aside to discuss the site's technical issues, policies, and operations.

The Village Pump is divided into four major sections: Policy, Technical, Proposals, and Miscellaneous. Click a section link to view a list of pages within each section.

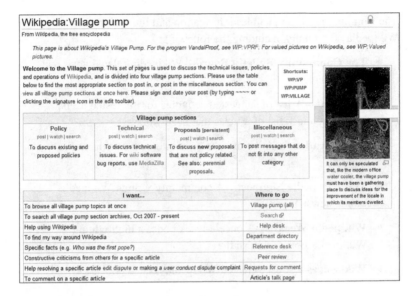

**FIGURE 20.2**    The Village Pump discussion page.

Each section is a Wikipedia page, and you add your voice to the discussion by editing the page and inserting your own comments. You can do this by clicking the Edit link next to a topic on the page, or by clicking the Edit This Page link at the top of the page. You insert your edits into the resulting edit box, using Wiki Markup Language as necessary.

> **NOTE: Wiki Markup Language**
> Learn more about the Wiki Markup Language in Lesson 9, "Editing an Existing Article."

# Other Ways to Communicate

The Community Portal and Village Pump are only two ways to communicate with the Wikipedia community—but they're not the only ways. Read on to learn more.

## Discussion Pages

Every article on the Wikipedia site has its own discussion page. This page is a wonderful place to interact with other users, in the context of improving the article in question. Participating in a discussion is as easy as clicking the Discussion tab at the top of the article page and then using the edit box to enter your comments and questions.

> NOTE: **Discussions**
>
> Learn more about discussions in Lesson 8, "Discussion an Article."

## User Pages

Every registered Wikipedia user has his or her own user page, like the one shown in Figure 20.3. You access your own user page by clicking your user name at the top of any Wikipedia page (after you've signed in, of course). The first time you do this, you should click the Start the User:*Username* Page link; this displays the edit page for your user page. Enter whatever it is you want to offer into the edit box; then click the Save Page button.

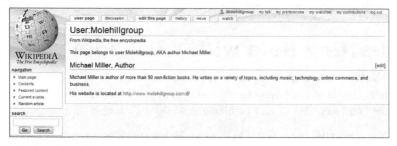

**FIGURE 20.3**   A typical Wikipedia user page.

> CAUTION: **Not a Personal Page**
>
> Your Wikipedia user page is not a personal web page and should not be used to display personal content. It should be reserved for Wikipedia-related discussions.

When your user page is created, other members of the Wikipedia community can leave comments by editing the page. You respond to their comments by doing further editing, and so on and so forth.

Similarly, you can enter into discussions on other user pages. To search for a user, enter the query **User:*Username*** into the Wikipedia search box. When you reach a user's page, click the Discussion tab to view comments from other readers; then click the Edit This Page tab to enter your comments on the discussion page.

## Mailing Lists

The Wikimedia Foundation maintains interactive mailing lists for all its sites, including Wikipedia. If you'd like to join the mailing list for the English-language Wikipedia (and participate in list-based discussions), go to lists.wikimedia.org/mailman/listinfo/wikien-l.

> PLAIN ENGLISH: **Mailing List**
> On the Internet, a discussion list distributed via email, where any subscriber can respond to the mailing and thus participate in the ongoing discussion.

# Getting Help with Wikipedia

The Wikipedia community is a great place to seek advice and ask questions. But if you're having trouble using the Wikipedia site, you can probably find solutions to your problems in Wikipedia's Help system.

You access the Help system by clicking Help in the Interaction panel of the Wikipedia navigation pane. When the Help:Contents page appears, as shown in Figure 20.4, you can browse for help on individual topics, or search for help by entering a query into the search box. Help content displays as a series of Wikipedia articles—which means the Help system itself is a collaborative effort of the Wikipedia community!

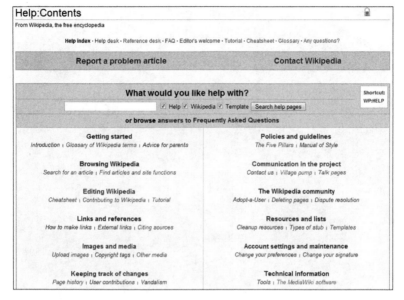

**FIGURE 20.4**   Wikipedia's main Help page.

# Summary

In this lesson, you learned how to participate in the Wikipedia community. In the next lesson, you learn to access Wikipedia from your iPhone.

# LESSON 21

# Using Wikipedia on Your iPhone

*In this lesson, you learn how to access Wikipedia from Apple's iPhone or iPod Touch.*

## Wikipedia on Safari

Apple's iPhone is one of the best-selling smartphones on the market today. One of its key selling points is the built-in Web browsing, via either WiFi (when available) or 3G cellular service.

> NOTE: **iPod Touch**
> The iPod Touch has the same Safari-based Web browsing capabilities as its iPhone sibling, but without 3G mobile phone capability. (It connects to the Internet via WiFi only.)

Web browsing is done via the built-in Safari Web browser. You can use Safari to access Wikipedia on your iPhone; just enter **en.wikipedia.org** into Safari's address box. As you can see in Figure 21.1, Wikipedia articles are formatted slightly differently on your mobile device than they are on your computer; the layout is adjusted for the size and shape of the iPhone screen.

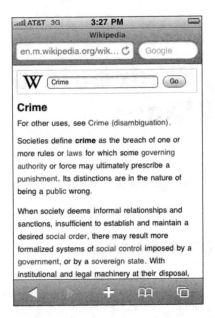

**FIGURE 21.1**   A Wikipedia article viewed on the iPhone.

NOTE: **Mobile Web**

If you look closely at the actually URL the iPhone uses to connect to Wikipedia, you see that it looks like this: **en.m.wikipedia.org.** That extra "m-dot" instructs Wikipedia to display a version of its pages enhanced for mobile devices.

TIP: **Mobile Wikipedia**

If you want to display a mostly text-only version of Wikipedia, best-suited for smartphones with smaller screens, enter **mobile.wikipedia.org** into your phone's browser.

# Wikipedia Applications

Several Wikimedia applications are available for the iPhone. These applications provide enhanced display and navigation, above and beyond what you get by accessing Wikipedia via the Safari Web browser.

Two of the most popular Wikipedia applications are discussed next. You find and download these applications from the iPhone App Store. To find Wikimedia applications, follow these steps:

1. Tap the App Store icon on the iPhone main screen.

2. When you connect to the App Store, tap the Search icon at the bottom of the screen.

3. Enter **wikipedia** into the search box; then tap the Search button.

4. When you find the application you want, tap it's name in the list.

5. Click the Free or price button; then tap Install.

6. Enter your iTunes password when prompted; then tap OK.

The application will now be downloaded to your iPhone.

## Wiki Mobile

Wiki Mobile provides a simplified interface for searching Wikipedia, as well as icons that let you view your Wikipedia history, save Wikipedia pages as bookmarks, and easily view other-language versions of the Wikipedia site.

One of the unique features of Wiki Mobile is that articles are initially displayed in a compressed format. That is, individual sections of the article are folded under each section's title, as shown in Figure 20.2; click a title to view the text for that section.

Wiki Mobile costs $1.99. Learn more at www.comoki.com/wikipedia/.

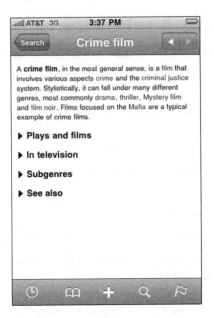

**FIGURE 21.2**   The Wiki Mobile application.

# Wikipanion

Wikipanion formats its pages differently from other Wikipedia applications and from the mobile version of Wikipedia. Instead of displaying images on separate lines from accompanying text, Wikipanion application places article images in line with the article text, similar to the way they display on your computer. For this reason, you might want to turn your iPhone 90 degrees to view the articles in widescreen, as shown in Figure 20.3.

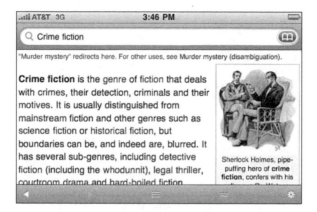

**FIGURE 21.3**  The Wikipanion application.

Also unique to Wikipanion is the Related button at the bottom of the screen. Tap this button to view a list of related topics and articles. You can view the table of contents for an article by tapping the Contents button at the bottom of the screen.

Wikipanion is available in both a free and a paid version; the paid version, Wikipanion Plus, costs $4.99. Learn more at www.wikipanion.net.

# Summary

In this lesson, you learned how to connect to Wikipedia on your iPhone. Now you can research with Wikipedia from just about anywhere—providing you have a cell phone connection!

# Index

# K

keywords, 25

Kovitz, Ben, 5

# L

languages, different-language versions, 21-22

licensing, 96-97

linking

to versions of articles, 55

to Wikipedia

*creating links, 154-155*

*reasons for, 153-154*

# M

mail lists, 168

media, finding in Wikimedia Commons, 97

browsing, 98-99

searching, 99

media files

uploading, 87-88

using in articles, 101

viewing, 99-100

MediaWiki, 9

mobile.wikipedia.org, 172

MP3 files, 92

# N

navigating Wikipedia

A-to-Z Index, 18

Featured Content, 15-16

glossaries, 20-21

main page, 11-15

outlines, 19-20

timelines, 19

topic portals, 16-17

news feed, 57

notability, 6, 79

## W-X-Y-Z

# FREE Online Edition

Your purchase of **Sams Teach Yourself Wikipedia® in 10 Minutes** includes access to a free online edition for 45 days through the Safari Books Online subscription service. Nearly every Sams book is available online through Safari Books Online, along with more than 5,000 other technical books and videos from publishers such as Addison-Wesley Professional, Cisco Press, Exam Cram, IBM Press, O'Reilly, Prentice Hall, and Que.

**SAFARI BOOKS ONLINE** allows you to search for a specific answer, cut and paste code, download chapters, and stay current with emerging technologies.

## Activate your FREE Online Edition at www.informit.com/safarifree

> **STEP 1:** Enter the coupon code: HSSEREH.

> **STEP 2:** New Safari users, complete the brief registration form. Safari subscribers, just log in.

If you have difficulty registering on Safari or accessing the online edition, please e-mail customer-service@safaribooksonline.com